THE FLYING CIRCUS

BY GARTH WALLACE

Published by
Happy Landings

Smile on!
Garth

Other books by Garth Wallace:

Fly Yellow Side Up
Pie In The Sky
Derry Air
Blue Collar Pilots
Don't Call Me a Legend

Canadian Catalogue Data:

The Flying Circus
fiction, aviation, humor

Written by:
Wallace, Garth 1946 -

ISBN 0-969-7322-6-0

C813'.54

Editing:
Liz Wallace
Sari Funston

Cover Art:
Francois Bougie

Typesetting and proofreading:
Amadeo Gaspar

Written, typeset, printed and bound
in Canada

Published by:

Happy Landings
RR #4
Merrickville, Ontario
K0G 1N0
Tel.: 613-269-2552
Fax: 613-269-3962
E-mail: books@happylanding.com
Web site: www.happylanding.com

THE FLYING CIRCUS

CONTENTS

INTRODUCTION

When airplanes and people come together, funny things can and do happen. I know; I taught flying for 19 years. Every day I met new characters and saw comedy unfold. Reflections of those times are in this book. Resemblance of people and stories to real life has been unavoidable but is included fondly and without malice. I hope you enjoy them as I have.

DEDICATION

The Flying Circus is dedicated to Eloise and Gord Henderson and Marg and Bill Alton. These are real people, the kind who anyone would be lucky to meet and to know.

The first two taught me that grace and humility are important in human relations and can be easily applied with practise. They practised every day to great effect.

Marg and Bill showed me how to really laugh: how to laugh readily, laugh easily, laugh long and laugh hard. "Life is too short for anything else," they said. They were right.

Thank you,
Garth Wallace

About the Author

Garth Wallace is from St. Catharines, Ontario, near Niagara Falls, where he learned to fly in a Fleet Canuck in 1966. From 1971 until 1990, Garth worked full time at various locations as a flying instructor, bush pilot and corporate pilot. It was during those flying years that he met the colorful characters and lived the humorous experiences that are the basis for his five books of funny flying stories. Garth now lives near Ottawa, Ontario with his wife Liz. He works as a publisher for the Canadian Owners and Pilots Association and flies a Grumman/American Trainer for pleasure.

About the Artist

Francois Bougie's interest in aviation was sparked at an early age by his father who restored several aircraft and constructed two homebuilts. Francois' passion led to a college education as an aircraft maintenance engineer and a career as an electromechanical designer in the aerospace industry in Montreal, Quebec. In the 1990s, Francois began applying an artistic talent to aviation art and industrial technical illustrations. His work has been published on several aviation book covers, posters and in aviation magazines. Francois is a licenced pilot. He has owned a Cessna 120 and a Pitts Special. He currently flies a classic 1946 Globe Swift that he restored.

Chapter One

THE FLYING CIRCUS

Barney Swallow sat hunched over an old government-issue oak desk. He was dressed in a brown tweed jacket and regiment tie that had seen too many drinks and not enough laundry. He looked like a crusty old veteran. Wild grey hair grew out of his eyebrows, ears and nose. His wrinkled, pocked face was a visual history of hard use and poor maintenance.

"So you want to lease some land." Barney's dentures whistled and clicked when he spoke.

"Yes sir, we do," I replied.

"How many people will you be employing?" The voice was low and gravelly.

Henry Rains and I were trying to start our own flying school in the City of Circus. Barney was the Circus Airport manager. My partner and I looked at each other. The two of us were going to do all the work ourselves at first.

"None," I replied.

"Wrong answer," he said staring at me through a pair of red-rimmed, runny eyes. He drew a raspy, deep breath. "You want me to go to council and secure you a favorable lease on airport property." It was a statement, not a question. "We have to do better than that. You're employing yourselves; that's two. You're helping to maintain my job; that's three. You'll be buying gas, meals, cleaning supplies and who knows what else from local merchants; that's ten. And you'll hire a couple of students to work the ramp; that's twelve."

"How much money will you be investing?"

I did some mental calculations. Henry and I were planning to put together $25,000 each; his from an inheritance, mine from a second mortgage. It represented half of what we needed. We were planning to borrow the rest of the money as a business loan from the bank.

Before I could answer, Barney spoke for me. "You said

Barney rose from his chair without straightening up. The meeting was over.

you're going to build a hangar, that's $100,000; buy two air-planes, they're worth $50,000; you'll need cars to get to work, clothes, pencils, and toilet paper, that's another $50,000; and then there will be your own sweat equity during the first few years, that comes to $250,000. We'll make it $260,000 and that doesn't include your expansion during the second five-year plan."

He was way ahead of us but the tone of his voice indicated that interruptions, comments or objections were not being entertained.

Barney opened his desk drawer, pulled out a dog-eared business card and pushed it in my direction. "That's Myrtle, my sister-in-law's answering service. That makes thirteen staff."

The card said, "EAVESDROPPERS, We listen while you work, Myrtle Knickenbacher".

"When you're ready to hire students," Barney continued, "I've got nephews."

He rose from his chair without straightening up and offered a handshake. The meeting was obviously over. "Council meets next Tuesday," he said. "Another week and you'll have your lease."

Henry and I were afraid of losing our instructing jobs before we

8

could open the doors of our own flying school. There were a million things to do. We had to obtain government operating certificates, borrow money, build a hangar and office, buy airplanes, hire a mechanic and promote the business. A premature loss of income would have been a tough setback.

Our wives had been the only ones who knew of our plans until we had visited the manager at the Circus Airport. The day after, our boss where we worked in nearby Derry, Irving Mingy, summoned the two of us to his office. He closed the door. "What are you calling your new flying school?" he asked straight out.

I was shocked. How could he know? Henry was ready. He looked Mingy square in the eye, "The Flying Circus," he said.

"I like it," Mingy said. "I'll lease you two Cherokees to help you get started."

"Why would you do that?" I blurted out. "We were trying to keep it a secret so you wouldn't fire us."

Mingy ignored me and looked at Henry. "He's a good instructor," he said, nodding his head in my direction, "but he has a lot to learn about business." Then he turned to me and spoke with an exaggerated patience. "I'm going to lease you two airplanes because they are old and tired. I know you'll take better care of them in your own business than you do here. This way they make me money so I can afford to get new ones. I don't fire you because I don't have replacement instructors - yet. I've arranged for you to work here until you get an Operating Certificate for your school and we get more staff. Angel will help you with the government paperwork. When you start, the airplanes come here for maintenance. It'll keep my shop busy. I've already arranged it. Any questions?"

I couldn't speak. Stingy Mingy had just cleared away half the hurdles that had blocked the path to starting our own flying school.

"No, sir," Henry said for us. He stood up and shook Mingy's hand. "Thank you very much."

"Welcome to long hours, high stress and hard work," Mingy said. "Now get out of here, get back on the job and take your buddy with you."

"Yes sir!" Henry replied.

"One more thing," Mingy said as we turned to go. "It's Irving from now on. We're partners."

"Yes, Sir Irving," Henry replied with a grin.

Irving waved us out of the room.

9

Chapter Two

BEHIND EVERY SUCCESSFUL MAN

My wife Susan had been very supportive of the flying school venture. I was lucky to have her for a mate. I was trading a steady income as a flying instructor at Derry Air for the chance of no income and the guarantee of a large debt. We had purchased an old farm the year before. Susan taught English riding at home part time. It was her escape from a high-pressure day job as manager of a ladies wear store in Derry. We had built stalls for several horses in the barn. It was logical that an indoor riding arena was the next thing on her mind but it went unmentioned when I told her about the potential flying school venture with Henry.

We had sat up late one night and talked about the opportunity: at least I talked and Susan listened. She tucked her long legs under her housecoat while I expounded on the joys of running a flying school. "The airport at Circus is smaller. There are no scheduled airline flights. It will be grass roots aviation at its best," I had said excitedly. "Beside teaching flying, we'll have barbecues, air rallies and film nights." I had also talked about the financial risk.

"I'm making good money," she had replied, "and we're young. If we're going to do something like this, it should be now. Start your flying school."

"I love you." It was all that I had left to say.

"I love you too. Now it's one o'clock in the morning and I'm going to bed."

"I'm wide awake," I said.

She gave me a kiss. "Good night sky pilot."

"Good night."

I turned the lights out and sat in the kitchen for another hour.

Our German Shepherd dog, Lady, slept at my feet while my mind raced with thoughts about starting a flying school.

Henry and I had met several years earlier. Our paths had crossed a few times until we were instructing together at Derry Air. We were the same age and had similar ideas when it came to instructing. We became good friends. Henry had received a small inheritance which triggered the idea that we start a flying school together. We had watched our boss, Stingy Mingy, make good money on the backs of his flying instructors.

Henry was a good candidate for a partner. He was the quiet, practical, plodding type: steady as a rock, handy, street smart and a really good flying instructor. We had agreed that he would be the flying school manager and maintenance coordinator.

I was not so steady, handy or smart but I had just as much instructing experience. It would be my job to sell the flying. I was the designated chief flying instructor although it didn't really matter what we called ourselves since we both had to do all the work.

11

It had been unbelievably easy for me to borrow money to match Henry's investment from his inheritance. I applied for a second mortgage on our farm, Windy Acres. I thought the bank manager would want a pile of paperwork including financial projections for the new business.

"No," he had said focusing on Susan's salary. "Your wife is making enough money to cover it. Get her to co-sign and the money is yours at four per cent over prime."

At the time, the prime rate was eight and a half per cent. Our first mortgage was at nine per cent.

Henry and I took our business plan to a bank in Circus. We wanted to build a good-sized hangar and office to show potential customers that we were solidly in business. We planned to put up half the money for the buildings and borrow the other half. The bank would be first in line for the full value of everything if we defaulted. It couldn't lose.

"Are you sure that's all you need?" the Circus bank manager had said. "Do you want more for start-up money?"

"Some of our customers from our previous jobs will be following us to the new school," Henry had said. "We'll be fine."

"Okay," the manager had replied. "The money is here whenever you're ready."

Barney Swallow came through with the land lease on the airport. We contracted to have an all-metal hangar built and in the process learned the first rule of the construction business: double your original cost estimate. The building went over budget. We had to stop construction before it was completed. We were left with an 80 by 80-foot steel shell with a 50-foot hole in the front for a door. We saved enough money for gravel on the hangar floor and the taxiway but there was no pavement. Instead of building offices, we bought a small display building from a bankrupt lumberyard and had it moved beside the hangar.

Mingy was true to his word. He leased us two Piper Cherokee 140s. Angel, his receptionist, prepared our applications for National Transportation Licences and Transportation Operating Certificates. She also wrote our operation and maintenance manuals while Henry and I continued to instruct and collect paycheques.

12

When the licences were issued we bid our goodbyes to Derry Air and flew the Cherokees to Circus.

So we were in business for better or worse. It was time to celebrate. Susan and I met Henry and his wife Leanne at a restaurant for dinner. We splurged on a bottle of wine and toasted our new flying school.

"We should think about promoting the business," I suggested.

"Are you going to advertise in the newspaper?" Susan asked.

"It's too expensive," I replied. "We'd be spending hundreds of dollars to promote $25 Introductory Flying Lessons. It's a hard way to get our money back."

"How about radio advertising or local cable TV?"

"It costs even more than the newspapers ads, Susan," I replied. "And they want you to buy a whole package."

"We could make up handbills," Henry said, "and put them on all the windshields at the golf clubs and marinas."

"Until we get arrested for trespassing and littering," I replied.

Leanne spoke up. "Advertise in the classifieds," she said.

We all gave her funny looks.

"Who reads the classifieds?" I asked.

"I do," she replied.

"There isn't a section for flying lessons," Henry said.

"There are other sections," she said.

"I thought people read the classifieds when they were looking for a specific item or service," Susan said.

"Think about what we are selling," Leanne offered. "You say 'flying lessons and airplanes' but that's not what we're selling. We're selling adventure. People learn to fly to escape from everyday life. The lessons are a challenge, a chance to make new friends and share an extraordinary accomplishment at the same time. Flying small airplanes is traveling to new places in a new way."

I didn't know Leanne very well. The four of us had spent several evenings together at the Rains' house over the last four months planning the flying school but she had never said very much. Her sudden business advice came as a surprise.

"You're right Leanne," Henry said, "but how do we advertise those things in the classifieds?"

"In the 'Personal' column," Leanne said. The three of us laughed in unison but Leanne stood her ground. "I knew you'd laugh but that section has one of the highest readerships in the newspaper."

13

"Come on, Leanne," I said. "The personals are full of lonely hearts, substance abuse salvation and rides to the west coast. Nobody reads that stuff."

"You obviously have," she replied. "Each personal classified ad is a mental adventure. The readership is much broader than the people who respond. Placing a 'Learn to Fly' ad there would be unique."

"She has a point," Susan said.

"Twenty-five words or less costs $8 a day for three days," Leanne added.

Henry and I looked at each other.

"Try it," Susan said.

"Sure, why not," I replied, "but our answering machine will be filled with bleeding hearts and druggies looking to get high."

"Hey," Henry said, "who cares as long as they want to fly."

Chapter Three

UNLIKELY PROSPECTS

"It's an old couple's car," I said. Henry and I were watching a boat-sized beige Buick cruise into our parking lot. An older couple climbed out.

"I'll bet they made a wrong turn on their way to a lawn bowling tournament," I said.

"You never know," Henry answered slowly and calmly.

I was being skeptical but it was for a good reason. It was opening day for our flying school. The euphoria of starting our own venture had masked the need for pessimism, until this morning. Our classified advertisements in the newspaper hadn't started. We were in danger of spending our first day without a customer.

The man and lady walking toward the office didn't look like candidates for flying lessons. The man was medium-sized and slightly bent with age. His soft shoes, pastel pants, polo shirt and cardigan sweater made him look like an older Bing Crosby. His thinning, grey hair was partially hidden by an out-of-date Ivy League cap. He appeared more ready to retire, than fly.

The woman could have passed for anybody's elderly aunt. Her jewelry and clothes were upscale, mismatched and loose fitting on a slight frame. Her wispy hair was cut short in an unsuccessful attempt to look modern. Her make-up needed to be rubbed into her cheeks. She looked like she had come for tea.

"So I'll handle this?" I asked Henry.

"That's right. You do the talking, Mister Promoter," he replied. "I'll listen and learn."

When Bing Crosby and his bride walked through the door, I shot them an insurance salesman's smile and then accidentally blurted out what was on my mind.

"Hello there. Are you lost?"

Blame it on nervousness or sudden cold feet brought on by the pressure of the last four months. As soon as it came out, I realized that it was a mistake.

15

My blunt greeting produced dead silence. Henry filled it. "Hi. I'm Henry Rains. Welcome to the Flying Circus."

They answered at the same time.

"I'm Glenn Hathaway," the man said.

"I'm Margaret Hathaway," his wife said.

Each offered Henry a handshake.

"Pleased to meet you," Henry said pumping their arms one at a time. "This is my partner," he said motioning in my direction.

"Pleased to meet you both," I said.

"Likewise," they replied together.

There was another silence while the couple stared at the wall and the ceiling panels in our office.

"Don't mind the lack of decorating," I said, trying to distract them. "We'll have some pictures up here in no time."

Each ceiling tile, floor tile and wall panel in our former lumber company display building was different. It was a bewildering mix to first-time viewers.

"Can I sell you folks some flying lessons?" Henry asked.

Glenn Hathaway was the next to speak. "Couldn't make up your mind on the decor?" he asked and then smiled at his own joke. "We learned to fly at the flying club next door," he added in answer to Henry's question. "We heard a new operation was starting so we came to see it."

"Tire kickers," I thought to myself.

"We have a number of aircraft for sale," Henry offered calmly.

I didn't know what he was talking about. All that we had were the two beat-up leased Cherokees. We had talked about buying a new airplane to get a jump on the competition but we knew from the Piper brochures that we couldn't afford one. Anyway, it didn't matter what Henry said. These senior citizens would not be in the market for an airplane.

"We are interested in our own aircraft," Glenn Hathaway said, "but the flying club staff don't know anything about aircraft sales."

I couldn't believe it.

Margaret Hathaway opened her purse and took out some swatches of fabric. "I brought samples of the material that we wanted for the upholstery," she offered.

Henry reached for the Piper brochures.

"What type of airplane did you have in mind?" he asked.

"Nothing too complicated," Glenn replied.

16

"Something for instrument flying," Mrs. Hathaway said at the same time. "We want to get our IFR Ratings."

My jaw dropped in disbelief.

"Have a seat," Henry said, motioning to one of the briefing tables. "Maybe I can talk my partner into making coffee."

I closed my mouth and did my bidding. Henry showed them the Piper Aircraft brochures. I still couldn't believe they were legitimate airplane customers. I used two scoops of coffee and five cups of water to save money.

"A Piper Archer might fit your needs," Henry said. "It's a four-place airplane, like the Warriors that you learned on at the flying club but comes with a larger, 180-horsepower engine. It can be equipped for instrument flying."

He showed them the instrument panel options and the interior brochure. "A variety of colors are available," he said, "in a woven fabric or a synthetic crushed velour."

"Does it come with an autopilot?" Mrs. Hathaway asked with a smile. "I like to fly, but Glenny loves the cruise control in his car."

"Yes," Henry replied, "a single-axis autopilot is standard with the dual IFR radio package."

They both looked through the brochures.

"I'll call the Piper distributor and ask about availability and prices," Henry said. "While I'm doing that, my partner can show you around outside." He gave me a nod.

I thought the tour outside was a bad idea. There were things unfinished. The hangar stood as a naked shell. There was gravel where there should have been asphalt and mud in place of landscaping.

"Watch your step," I said as I led the Hathaways out of the office and onto a gravel path. "We haven't had time to plant grass or lay the sidewalk," I said, "but the hangar is up. We hope to finish it soon."

It was the first of May. The sky was clear and the weather was warming up to the promise of a summer soon to come.

We walked to the front of the hangar. Our two leased Cherokee 140s were the only things inside. They looked forlorn parked in the middle of the big open space.

"When we get time, we're going to have lights installed and a door," I explained.

Henry and I had worked on the things that hadn't cost money but I felt stupid making excuses for the things we couldn't afford. I had the blisters to prove that we had raked and rolled the gravel and the dirt around the buildings. We had scrubbed the two old Cherokees inside and out but the hangar and property still had that "under construction" look.

Glenn and Mrs. Hathaway walked over to the airplanes and peaked through the cockpit windows of each one. The only other thing I could think to show them was our fuel installation. The flying club, our competitors on the field, held the airport fuel concession. It had been Henry's idea to find a couple of used furnace oil tanks and pump our own fuel by hand. We had painted the two tanks with a roller and a brush. They stood in the mud beside the gravel taxiway as a monument to our budget operation.

"What do you charge for hangar space for an Archer?" Glenn Hathaway asked.

Henry and I hadn't set hangar rates.

"I don't know," I said, "but we can figure it out for you." It was a lame answer.

We went back inside the office where Henry offered the Hathaways a coffee.

We went back inside the office where Henry offered the Hathaways a coffee.

"Cream and two sugar," Glenn said.

"Just black," Mrs. Hathaway said at the same time.

When the coffee was poured, Henry said that he had spoken to the Piper distributor. "They don't have an Archer in stock. It would have to be specially ordered."

They spoke in unison. "We wanted to do that anyway," Glenn said. "We'd like to order our own paint colors and interior."

"We want to visit the factory while our airplane is being built," Mrs. Hathaway said.

"Fine," Henry replied. "I priced an Archer with the dual radios and the executive option package. Delivery would be three months following a deposit of $5,000."

"How about insurance?" Glenn asked.

Henry quoted him what I recognized to be the cost of the insurance on our two old Cherokees together. "That's a ballpark figure," he said. "I can get a quote from our own insurance agent."

"What would it cost to park it in your hangar?" Glenn asked.

"One hundred dollars per month," Henry said without hesitation.

"What about maintaining an Archer?"

"It will come with a two-year warranty. There will be the labor costs on an inspection every 100 hours of flying or one year, whichever comes first. We have an arrangement with a maintenance base in Derry. A mechanic will come here if necessary."

"Well, we appreciate the information," Glenn said. "Margaret and I will talk it over and let you know."

"Thank you for coming," I said.

"Since you're here," Henry interjected, "my partner and I are available to fly your first instrument lesson on our Cherokees this morning."

The Hathaways exchanged surprised looks.

"It involves a half-hour ground briefing and a one-hour flight," Henry continued. "We have two airplanes and two experienced instructors. You'd be finished by noon."

Glenn gave him a hard look, "Let me get this straight. You're offering Margaret and me a lesson right now?"

"That's correct," Henry replied. "The cost is $15 an hour for the ground briefing and $55 an hour each in the aircraft, instructor

19

included. The first five instrument lessons are the same as the first five hours of the night flying rating. You'll be working on both ratings at once. We could also count it as a checkout on our aircraft. You could rent them while deciding on your purchase."

"I've never been offered a flying lesson that I didn't have to book weeks in advance," Glenn said.

"Well," Henry said with a smile, "you can book it ahead if you prefer but my partner and I are ready to work. We'd rather take you now."

"I'd like to go flying now," Mrs. Hathaway said.

"Fine," Henry replied and nodded to me. "I'll get the airplanes ready and you do the ground briefing."

"Okay," I replied.

I had obviously hooked up with the right partner.

"Bring your coffee over here, folks," I said with new-found enthusiasm, "and I'll show you what we're going to do today."

Chapter Four

THE LITTLE OLD LADY
FROM CIRCUS

Glenn and Mrs. Hathaway sat in front of the blackboard we had nailed to the end wall of the office. I used it and a cockpit photo from a Piper brochure to review the function of each flight instrument. They both listened politely. Glenn answered most of my questions. I decided his wife was a tag-along spouse supporting her husband's hobby with her attendance but not with her attention or her interest.

When we were done, Henry signed himself out with Glenn. "I've done the pre-flight checks on both aircraft," Henry said, "so we can climb in and go flying."

"You mean we don't have to do our own walkarounds while the instructors wait in the office and drink coffee?" Glenn asked.

"We're trying to make a good first impression," Henry replied with a smile.

"I'm impressed already," Glenn said, returning the smile.

Henry had pulled both airplanes from the hangar and left them parked one behind the other on the taxiway. He and Glenn Hathaway headed for the lead Cherokee. Mrs. Hathaway and I walked to the second.

Mrs. Hathaway climbed onto the catwalk of the low-wing Cherokee, opened the right hand door and slid over to the left seat with better agility that I expected for an older lady in a skirt. Once installed, she started rummaging in her handbag. I sat down in the right seat and held the door ajar for fresh air. She pulled out a tissue and tucked it up the right sleeve of her sweater.

"In case a girl gets the sniffles," she offered.

I nodded.

The engine started in the Cherokee ahead of us. Mrs. Hathaway reached into her purse again and extracted a tube of lipstick and a compact mirror.

21

"It's part of my pre-start check," she said with a little smile.

I'd never seen it on an aircraft checklist. "Take your time," I said.

She finished applying the lipstick. "Girls my age have to use everything they can to look good." She gave me a bigger smile.

She dropped the lipstick tube back into the purse and dug out a bag of scotch mints. "Candy?" she offered.

They smelled good. "Yes, thank you," I replied.

The other Cherokee started to taxi toward the runway. Mrs. Hathaway then pulled a pair of half-round reading glasses on a string from her purse. I must have looked impatient.

"I'll be ready to go in a minute," she said.

"There's no hurry," I lied.

It looked like we were going to spend the whole hour getting ready. Glenn Hathaway and Henry were already beside the runway doing a pre-take-off check in the other aircraft.

There was a checklist in our aircraft side pocket but Mrs. Hathaway pulled her own from the purse. "Do you mind if I use this one?" she asked. "I'm more familiar with it from when I learned to fly."

At the rate we were going, it didn't matter what she used, we were never going to get airborne.

"It's fine," I said politely.

"Thank you."

The little old lady immediately started running down the pre-start list rapidly and out loud. She sounded like an auctioneer. In a matter of seconds she was through the check. She pumped the throttle, yelled "Clear!" out the pilot's side vent window and turned the key. The engine fired, chugged and then settled into a smooth idle. She turned off the electric fuel pump, checked the engine gauges, snapped the radio on and called the ground controller.

"Good morning Mrs. Hathaway," the controller replied. "The runway is 24, wind 240 at 20 knots, altimeter 2992; you're cleared to taxi Charlie, Bravo to hold short of 24, call the tower for take-off."

She released the brakes. "Roger, and a cheery good morning to you," she replied brightly.

"Sounds like you're well known here," I commented.

She gave me a big smile. "The boys in the tower are friendly, but

I wish they'd call me Margaret."

While talking, Mrs. Hathaway/Margaret had been taxiing the airplane at a fast clip. She pulled up beside the runway and immediately started into a pre-take-off check. Henry and her husband were parked on the runway about to depart.

She smiled as she continued her rapid-fire run through the checks. "Seat belt on, door closed," she said to me. Without waiting for a reply, she spun the radio selector to the tower frequency and called for a take-off clearance.

The other airplane was rolling down the runway.

"Tango Victor Hotel, taxi into position and hold," the controller replied.

"Tango Victor Hotel."

"Victor Hotel is now cleared for takeoff, wind two four zero at twelve"

"Victor Hotel."

I just got the door closed and latched in time as Margaret accelerated onto the runway. She continued into the take-off roll all in one motion. At lift-off speed, she held the airplane on the ground. It continued to gain momentum. Her face was split with a wide grin. I was about to tell her to raise the nose when she hauled back on the control wheel and pulled the Cherokee into a steep, zooming climb that put us both on our backs. She turned to me and whooped, "I love doing this!"

The Cherokee's extra airspeed bled off. When it had decreased to the best rate of climb of 85 mph, Margaret pushed forward on the control wheel and held the airplane in level flight. She retracted the flaps and allowed the airspeed to build up.

The city of Circus lay before us and we were headed over the centre of it at 500 feet. Margaret saw the questioning look on my face. "The only time you can legally fly over the city this low is on takeoff or landing," she offered. "It's amazing what you can see in your neighbors' backyards from up here."

My opinion of this suddenly feisty and capable lady was improving quickly. When we had finished skimming over a large part of the city, I convinced Margaret to climb a couple of thousand feet. Once there, I demonstrated how to fly using the instruments as the only reference. She practised some basic manoeuvers without looking out of the window. She was good. We progressed quickly through the lesson.

23

About 45 minutes later, we heard Glenn call the Circus Control Tower asking for a clearance to re-enter the control zone. We headed back to the airport. Margaret set up a high-speed descent down to the approach altitude of 1,000 feet above the ground. She called the tower. We were cleared to the downwind leg to follow the other Cherokee. Margaret avidly watched the houses below as we flew over the city. When he had us in sight, the controller said we were number two for landing.

Margaret eased the Cherokee's nosewheel onto the centreline and held it there. The main wheels were still in the air.

Margaret completed a rapid-fire pre-landing check but continued to fly at high speed at 1,000 feet. We were soon too high and tight to the runway for a normal approach to landing. I didn't say anything. I could see the other Cherokee touching down. On the base leg of our approach, 90 degrees to the runway, Margaret cut the engine power. Then she applied full right rudder and most of the left aileron, dumping us into a crossed-control slipping turn to the left. We dropped like a rock. Her smile grew bigger. She straightened the airplane out on the final leg for the runway about a half kilometre back. The controller cleared us to land. We were no longer too high but we were flying at 120 mph.

I stayed silent. I was curious to see how Margaret was going to land the airplane at its top speed. Normal touchdown velocity was half of what we were doing. When we crossed the approach lights to Runway 24, the airplane had slowed to the maximum flap extension speed of 110 mph. Margaret hauled on the lever between the seats and extended full flaps. She nicely anticipated the resulting pitch up. We crossed the end of the runway doing 95 mph.

The next manoeuver was nearly impossible to do without porpoising down the runway. Margaret eased the Cherokee's nosewheel onto the centreline and held it there perfectly. The main wheels were still in the air. As the speed continued to bleed off, the main wheels settled onto the asphalt. When our speed had dropped below 75 mph, she squeezed the toe brakes without locking up the tires. The airplane was slowed down to a walk by the first taxiway. We turned off.

"Glenn hates it when I fly like that," she said, beaming. "Thank you, I enjoyed it."

"You had me on the edge of my seat," I replied.

"Oh, I'm sorry. I didn't mean to frighten you. My previous instructor usually fell asleep by the time we got back to the airport."

"Don't worry about me," I replied. "You fly the airplane very well."

"Thank you."

Margaret shut down the Cherokee on the ramp behind the other airplane. We joined Henry and Glenn in the office.

"I learned a lot today," Glenn was saying as Margaret and I walked in. "I appreciate your taking us up right away. I don't speak for Margaret but I'd like to book another lesson."

Henry was standing behind our small flight desk looking at the empty booking sheets. "Sure, anytime," he said calmly.

"Can we fly again Wednesday afternoon around two o'clock?" Glenn asked

"Yes," Henry said. "How about you, Mrs. Hathaway?"

"Margaret," she replied, "please call me Margaret and Wednesday will be fine."

"Okay, we'll fly with you both again on Wednesday at 14:00 for another hour and a half."

While Henry was making the bookings, Glenn pulled out his chequebook.

"Don't bother making us out a bill," Glenn said, writing out a cheque. "Here's $2,000. Put it on an account for us. Keep track of our lessons and let us know when we're running out."

He handed Henry the cheque. My partner didn't know what to say. Neither did I.

"And starting today," Glenn continued, "we'd like to start paying monthly hangar rent for a Piper Archer. On Wednesday I'll bring you a deposit and an order for the airplane."

Henry's mouth dropped open. Margaret nodded her agreement. I pinched myself to see if I was dreaming.

Henry recovered quickly. "I'll have the order form drawn up for Wednesday," he said, "but you don't have to pay hangar rent until the aircraft is delivered."

"That may be true," Glenn replied, "but I enjoy seeing energetic people starting in business. It reminds me of when Margaret and I opened our first hardware store. Charge our hangar rent starting now and I can brag that we were your first customers."

"Thank you very much," Henry said.

"You're welcome," Glenn replied, and then he added with a smile, "You should do fine but see if you can teach your partner how to make a decent cup of coffee."

"I'll work on it," Henry replied.

Chapter Five

SET UP

Two men in their early 50s walked into the Flying Circus office on the afternoon of our second day in business. They were dressed in slightly rumpled, workday suits and ties. They looked like farmers going to church. The first one was short and round like a bowling pin. He did all the talking.

"Hi, are you Henry Rains?" he asked. His expression and tone were friendly. His tall skinny partner smiled slightly.

I was sitting behind our flight desk filling in the aircraft logbooks from the previous day's flights. Henry was flying with Moose, one of the students that we had stolen from our former employer.

I stood up.

"No, I'm his partner," I replied, introducing myself. "Henry is up with a student. Welcome to The Flying Circus."

"I'm Al Milton," bowling pin said, "and this is Bruce Stanwick. Glenn Hathaway told us about this place. We were thinking of taking flying lessons."

I jumped at the chance to sharpen my salesmanship. "Well you came to the right place," I replied. "We offer a $25 introductory flying lesson. There's an aircraft available now. If you two gentlemen have time, I'll take you both flying and show you the first lesson. It'll take about an hour and a half."

"Okay," Al said, "as long as it's with you. Glenn warned us not to fly with your partner. He said you were okay but Rains was dull."

I hesitated a second. This guy was either joking or he had mistakenly switched Henry and me. Either way, I didn't correct him. I wanted to sell them flying lessons.

Al continued with a smirk, "He told us that Rains couldn't even make a decent cup of coffee."

"Henry and I are both well qualified flying instructors," I said, "but I'll be happy to take you up today."

"Glenn said you're the best," Al added and then chuckled. His tall partner just smiled.

"Well, let's go flying," I replied, "and you can decide that for yourself."

"Don't we need an IQ test or something first to see if we qualify to take lessons?" Al asked.

I hesitated again. It was a strange question.

"I won't have any trouble," he added, "but I'm worried about Bruce here." He laughed at his own joke. Bruce kept smiling.

"No," I replied, "learning to fly isn't that hard. You'll see when we go up."

"How about life insurance? Do you have one of those machines where Bruce can stick in a quarter and insure himself? Twenty-five cents is all he's worth."

By now Al was chuckling continuously as he spoke. He was obviously enjoying himself at his buddy's expense but Bruce kept smiling without saying anything.

I held a straight face.

"Flying is safe," I offered. "Glenn Hathaway will tell you that."

"Glenn? He's certifiably crazy," Al laughed. "He flies with that woman of his. He's gonna die for sure."

"I'll explain the course before we go up," I said, ignoring his last comment. I handed them each a copy of the Private Pilot outline.

Al glanced at it. "Do we need our own plane?" he asked.

"No," I replied. "This course outline shows the cost including a rental aircraft."

"Would we get a discount if we had our own plane?"

"Yes," I said hesitantly. No one had asked me that before. "You'd be charged for the instructor's time only. The cost of the rental aircraft would be knocked off the price."

Al turned to his buddy. "Wow, look here Bruce, we can save thousands."

"Except you'd have to pay the operating costs of your own aircraft," I added quickly.

"But if we owned it, we'd be paying those costs anyway," Al said, "and if we owned it together, the cost would be half. We'd save twice as much!"

The scary part of Al's fuzzy logic was that I understood it, but I didn't want to get sidetracked from the lesson.

"We can discuss aircraft ownership anytime," I said. "You keep those outlines and we'll go flying."

"This guy's smart," Al said to Bruce with a snort. "He wants to make money on his time and his airplanes."

28

"It's only got three wheels," he exclaimed. "What happened to the fourth?"

I signed us out, put a note on the door and led them to the hangar. When Al saw the Cherokee 140, he continued his stream of questions.

"It's only got three wheels," he exclaimed. "What happened to the fourth?"

"Airplanes are made to fly in the air, not on the roads," I explained patiently.

"There're no bumpers. What happens if we hit something?"

Al's questions were a nuisance but you had to like him. He always spoke with a laugh or at least a chuckle and a smile.

"We're going to be flying at 100 mph, Al," I replied. "If we hit anything, bumpers will be the last thing we need."

"Do we get parachutes?" he asked.

"No. Parachutes won't do us any good either. Airplanes only crash when they hit the ground. If that happens, it will be too late for a parachute."

29

The twisted logic of this answer seemed to satisfy him but only for a few seconds and then the questions continued. He asked why the wing was on the bottom and not the top; why the building was called a hanger when there was nothing hanging in it; and if the things on the wings were called ailerons, did he have to learn French to fly?

I soon realized that my answers didn't matter. As soon as he was done one question, Al was thinking ahead and asking about something else. Bruce continued to smile. He listened without saying a word. I kept my answers short in an effort to get airborne before the day was finished.

We pulled the Cherokee 140 out of the hangar. I installed Al in the left seat and Bruce in the back. I climbed into the right seat and started to explain the basic instruments and controls.

"Let me get this straight," Al said. "Canada is going metric but aviation is in knots except this airplane, which is in miles per hour because it's older?"

"That's right."

"And the altitude is in feet and pressure is in inches of Mercury."

"Yes."

He turned to Bruce. "This learning to fly is rigged. They've made it so complicated that this guy is going to be a millionaire on our money."

"Taken a bit at a time, none of this is complicated," I offered.

"That's easy for you to say," Al laughed. "You're getting paid by the hour."

I started the engine.

"Was this thing built in the 30s?" Al asked. "My dad had a Ford with a hand throttle like that."

I called the ground controller and we taxied out.

"My uncle had an old tractor that you steered with your feet," Al said.

"How come we have to make up names on the radio like `Tango and Victor and Hotel'? Why can't I say its Al Milton? How many Al Miltons can there be flying at the same time?"

I tried ignoring this last question.

Al turned to Bruce and whispered loudly, "He doesn't know."

I started to explain why we would be taking off into the wind.

"Now if I was walking into the wind, it would slow me down," Al said. "We could go faster with the wind."

30

I demonstrated the takeoff. Al continued to ask questions. Bruce continued to smile.

"How do we get traction with the tires hung in the air?"

"The propeller gives us traction."

"Why is it so noisy?"

"Don't worry about it," I replied, "until the noise stops."

Al liked my little joke. "If the engine stops and I die," he said with a chuckle, "I want my money back."

When we had leveled off from the climb, I let Al fly the aircraft. He sawed away on the controls like a youngster on a 25-cent supermarket kiddy ride. "Take it easy," I suggested, "the controls are very sensitive."

"I thought I was doing alright," Al replied. "What's the matter, are you going to be sick?"

He laughed at his own question and then he looked at Bruce in the back seat to see his reaction. Bruce wasn't smiling anymore. The rocky ride was getting to him.

I took over control and headed west. My intention was to land at Orville Kenny's place so Bruce and Al could switch seats. I also thought these farmer types would enjoy landing at a private grass airport. Seeing Orville's set-up might sell them on getting their pilot licences. I also wanted to speak to Orville about his flying lessons.

I had met Orville while working for the flying school in the town of Derry. The instructors at Derry practised off-airport approaches at Orville's landing strip. He was a successful farmer who loved airplanes. He had built the strip and then started taking flying lessons with me.

I explained the plan to Bruce and Al. Bruce nodded in agreement. Al continued to ask questions.

"Is this the Kenny family from north of Toronto?"

"I don't know," I replied, pointing at the airstrip below on Al's side.

"Who does this guy know that he can have his own airport?"

"Anyone with land can have an airport," I replied and set up an approach.

I described what I was doing all the way to the touchdown. The Cherokee 140 was a good off-airport airplane so I demonstrated what it could do. I knew Orville's strip was as smooth as asphalt but I used full flap and a minimum speed because it was early spring. The grass might have been soft.

31

We sailed over the wires at the beginning of the runway. I held the aircraft nose high and stalled it into the grass. It was a perfect soft field touch down but I had forgotten to warn Al that the stall horn would sound.

"Jesus priest, what was that?"

"Sorry Al," I said. "That's the high angle of attack warning. It indicates something that can be a problem if we're not close to touching down."

"It sounded like the fries were ready at McDonalds."

Orville was standing beside the parking area as we taxied toward the farmhouse.

"What kind of airplane does he have?" Al asked.

"He doesn't. He's just learning how to fly."

"Why would he turn all this land into a runway when he doesn't own an aircraft?"

"So friendly pilots like us can drop by for a visit."

With that I shut down the engine and opened the door.

"Good afternoon," I called out to Orville. "I brought a couple of new customers for you to meet."

"Welcome to Kenny's International," the friendly farmer said as he walked around the right wing tip.

I climbed out and introduced Al and Bruce as they exited the airplane.

That was the last thing that I said for a long time. Al took over. At first he circled Orville verbally, the way farmers do. He complimented the weather and then Orville's farm, which was easy since the land and buildings were immaculately kept. Orville was shy in his responses. Then Al got right into the nosey farmer stuff to find out who Orville was and who he knew.

It turned out that Al and Bruce lived on farms not far away. They grew grapes while Orville farmed for grain but they had friends and acquaintances in common. The floodgates of conversation opened wide. I tried more than once to end the visit by saying, "Well Orville, it's been good to see you." I was ignored.

Orville insisted that we tour the buildings and see his polished farm equipment. Bruce said nothing but the look on his face indicated that he was enjoying himself.

We went into the house "to meet the missus." The kitchen held the inviting smell of a bakery. Annabelle Kenny was introduced to Al and Bruce.

"You won't believe who they know," Orville said and then related most of our previous conversation.

"Lands sake," Annabelle exclaimed, "then you must know the Richardsons. Have a seat. I've some fresh pie and coffee and I don't take 'no' for an answer."

I could see the rest of my afternoon going down the drain. We were there for over an hour. The $25 introductory flying lesson turned into a loss leader for me. I could only hope the time invested would pay off in future business.

My efforts to wind up the visit had no effect until I mentioned that it was four o'clock. That put Al in a sudden hurry. I found out later that both men were government employees who lived in the country and farmed as a sideline. During the day Al worked as a health inspector and Bruce was an electrical foreman for Provincial Hydro. They were taking the introductory flying lesson on taxpayer time which ended at four o'clock. I also learned later from bachelor Bruce that Al was very married and was expected home at five o'clock with no excuses allowed.

I managed to book some time for Orville to finish his pilot licence at The Flying Circus before Al hustled us to the airplane. I put Bruce in the left seat and Al in the back. I started the Cherokee, waved to Orville and took off right from the parking spot. On the way to the airport I gave Bruce a chance to fly. He was a natural. Within seconds of taking the wheel, he had mastered the soft touch required to prevent over controlling. Al leaned forward between our shoulders.

"Did you see that Massey Harris four-wheel? Do you know what that unit is worth?"

"Now try a gentle turn to the left, Bruce," I said.

"That man must be growing money trees," Al continued. "Did he inherit all that from somebody or is 'she' rich?"

"Now turn back to the right, Bruce."

"Does that Orville guy work outside - maybe at a bank?"

"I don't know, Al. Okay, Bruce, now pitch the nose down and I'll reduce the power so we can descend toward the airport."

Al continued. "With the money he has tied up in that shed, Orville could buy both of our farms and have some left over to hire us to run them."

I called the Circus Control Tower as we approached the airport. Al jabbered away about Orville and farm equipment. He didn't notice that I was talking Bruce through the approach and the landing with just a little guidance on my dual control wheel.

Henry was in the office when we returned. I worried about Al blurting out a backward comment about Glenn Hathaway's recommendations for an instructor but I didn't know what to do about it. I introduced Henry to Al and Bruce.

"You're the guy that Glenn Hathaway told us to fly with," Al said and grinned. "Where were you earlier this afternoon? It took this guy three hours to give us a twenty-minute lesson."

Al looked at me and laughed. Bruce grinned. They had set me up.

Both men wanted more lessons. I suggested that they fly in separate aircraft to speed things up. I got even with Al by booking him with no-nonsense Henry.

Chapter Six

VIOLATED

When Melville was done transmitting, he'd look at me. If I nodded my approval, he'd release the mic button.

The air traffic controllers in the Circus Tower seemed friendly except for one. Mr. Miserable's tone on the radio contained all the warmth of a high school principal talking to the kid who set fire to the school. He was working the day I checked out Melville Passmore in one of our Cherokee 140s.

I had taught Melville to fly at my previous job at Derry Air. He followed as a customer to The Flying Circus. Melville looked like a Melville: short, round, a little grubby but farmer friendly. He hooked his thumbs under his coverall straps when he talked and left his tongue hanging out between sentences. He lived at home and helped his parents on their farm. He saved all his money for flying.

Melville had flown our Cherokees at Derry Air but that had been a while ago and at a different airport. I agreed to go with him for his first flight at Circus.

Melville was a good pilot but he didn't like talking on the radio. For him it was like public speaking. It terrified him. To transmit, Melville pressed the microphone button, took a deep breath, looked both ways, licked his lips as he hauled in his tongue and then spoke from a pre-written script on a kneeboard. He pushed the words up from his boots like a belch. When he was done transmitting, he'd look at me. If I nodded my approval, he'd release the mic button.

When we were ready to taxi, Melville went through his routine: mic on, breath in, look both ways, lick lips, tongue in and talk, "Circus Ground, this is Cherokee Foxtrot Tango Victor Hotel, request taxi instructions for circuits." He looked at me. I nodded. He released the button.

There was no response. We waited; still nothing. I tested the receive volume with the squelch. It was up. Melville looked at me to see what to do next. Before I could say anything, the voice of Mr. Miserable in the tower boomed through the aircraft cabin speaker.

"Tango Victor Hotel, did you copy?"

The controller had obviously talked before Melville had released the mic. We had missed it. His sharp tone struck instant fear into Melville.

"Say, 'Say again,'" I said.

Mic on, breath, look, tongue, "Say, say again," Melville said. He looked at me, I nodded, mic button released.

The controller growled, "I said, 'Did you copy the taxi instructions?'" This time the tone was beyond strict. It was threatening.

Melville looked at me. "Say, 'Negative,'" I said.

Melville went through his routine and then said, "Negative." He looked at me and I nodded. When he released the mic, the controller was part way through the instructions again.

"... altimeter three zero one zero, taxi via Charlie, Bravo."

I looked at the windsock. It showed the wind favored Runway 24 so I decided we could guess the rest of the clearance and leave the controller training for another day.

"Acknowledge with 'Tango Victor Hotel,'" I told Melville.

"Tango Victor Hotel?" he asked into the open microphone. I nodded. He let go.

"In future, Tango Victor Hotel, listen on the frequency for a reply after you make a transmission," the controller snapped.

Melville's eyes grew large as saucers.

"Don't reply," I advised him, "he's having a bad day."

We taxied out and did the pre-take-off checks. Melville asked for a take-off clearance. The controller launched into his reply before Melville released the mic button.

"... call on the downwind," was all we heard.

We could have guessed that it was the end of a take-off clearance but I didn't want to make a mistake with Mr. Miserable.

"Ask him to 'Say again,'" I said to Melville.

He didn't want to. Before he could depress the mic button the controller jumped on him.

"Did you copy the clearance Tango Victor Hotel?"

Melville went through his routine and said, "Say again, Circus tower."

This time the controller read the take-off clearance slowly and loudly. Each word dripped with sarcastic impatience.

Melville answered him, "Tango Victor Hotel." He looked at me. I nodded. He released the mic button.

"At least now he's working at our speed," I said to relieve some of the tension.

We did two circuits with touch and go landings and takeoffs with each one. Melville flew them perfectly. I picked up the microphone on the third downwind leg and said, "Tango Victor Hotel, downwind Runway 24, request Alpha."

"Tango Victor Hotel cleared touch and go Runway 24, wind 250, five to ten."

"Tango Victor Hotel."

"Request Alpha" was a code between flying schools and control towers that I had learned at my last job in Derry. It meant that I wanted the controller to give Melville instructions to practise an overshoot when he was on final approach to the runway. Using the code made it a surprise emergency procedure for the student.

Melville started on a base leg, set up a descent and then turned on final. I waited for the overshoot instruction. It never came. Melville executed another perfect touch and go. I decided that the controller must have forgotten to give it to us.

On the next downwind leg, I worked the microphone again. "Tango Victor Hotel, downwind Runway 24, request Bravo."

"Tango Victor Hotel cleared touch and go Runway 24, wind 240 at ten."

"Tango Victor Hotel."

"Request Bravo" indicated to the controller that I was going to pull the power back after the next takeoff to simulate an engine failure in the climb out. There was nothing for the controller to do. The code just warned him that the airplane was not experiencing a real engine failure so he didn't need to call the emergency vehicles.

Melville set up an approach. On final it looked like he was going to nail another good landing.

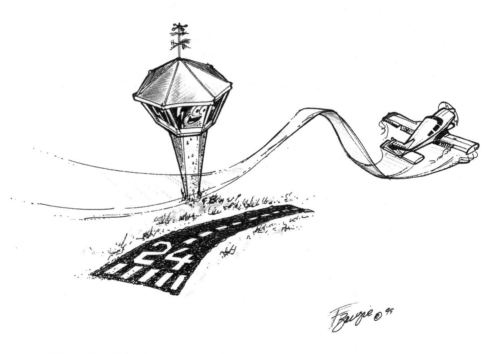

When the Cherokee was climbing off the far end of the runway, I reached for the throttle lever and pulled it back to idle.

"Tango Victor Hotel, pull up and go around, pull up and go around!" the controller barked, then he added, "practise only." His sour tone made it realistic.

Melville obeyed and executed a good missed approach. I thought it was a neat trick by the controller to wait an extra circuit before issuing the overshoot. He even had me surprised.

When the Cherokee was climbing off the far end of the runway, I reached for the throttle lever and pulled it back to idle. "Practise engine failure after takeoff," I declared to Melville.

The little farm boy pushed the airplane's nose down, set up a glide and leaned forward to look for an open area for landing. Most of the land off the end of Runway 24 belonged to a dairy. Melville headed the airplane toward a suitable piece of pasture. He knew the stubby-winged Cherokee 140 wouldn't glide far. He picked a field close by.

"Tango Victor Hotel, are you experiencing a problem?" The controller demanded over the cabin speaker.

I thought it was exceptionally realistic of him to add that transmission to our practise. Melville looked at me.

"What would you do in a real situation?" I asked.

"Fly the airplane."

"Correct, so fly the airplane."

Melville lined up on the field. The approach looked good. As we descended through 200 feet, I reapplied the power.

"Nice job, Melville. Rejoin the circuit and we'll practise a short field landing for a full stop."

"Tango Victor Hotel, are you experiencing a problem?" the controller demanded again.

The voice was so demanding I knew the transmission wasn't part of the practise emergency procedure.

"Negative," I replied.

"Is that Tango Victor Hotel responding?" the controller barked. There was no other traffic. He was being very picky.

"Affirmative, the 'negative' is from Tango Victor Hotel," I replied.

"Call downwind," he said sharply.

"Tango Victor Hotel."

I let Melville call for a full stop landing. He was cleared to land. He nailed a full flap, short field landing on the runway numbers. When we had turned onto the taxiway, Melville called ground control for clearance to the Circus ramp. It was the same controller working both positions. He cleared us in and then added sternly, "The pilot is to call the control tower when he gets in the office."

39

Melville looked at me. His eyes were at full wide. He had been around flying schools enough to know the controller's statement was bad news.

"In this case, Melville, I'm the pilot, you're the student."

I phoned the tower from the office. The controller was shouting mad.

"It didn't matter when you asked for an engine failure after takeoff and didn't do it but I had a big problem when you did it on the next circuit without asking!" the controller yelled. I held the telephone receiver away from my ear. Melville winced. Mr. Miserable continued his tirade. "I'm here for your sake, not for mine," he bellowed. "When an airplane goes down without indicating a practise, I'm obligated to call out the emergency response teams. I had my hand on the hot line when you pulled up from your practise."

While he was raging, I was running the sequence of circuits and procedures through my head. It was obvious to me that either he or I had the codes switched.

"If I had called for a response, you would be in bigger trouble, mister!"

He was making a mountain out of a molehill. I considered telling him that we had experienced an engine failure and corrected it in the nick of time but I decided that it might get me in bigger trouble.

"Where I come from," I offered as calmly as possible, "an 'Alpha' is a request for a practise overshoot and a 'Bravo' is a notice of a practise engine failure after takeoff."

"Well you're not where you come from!" the controller said with a blast. "Here an 'Alpha' is a requested practise engine failure and 'Bravo' is a requested overshoot."

"That's good to know," I said, "thank you."

"Go ahead your name and pilot licence number," the controller demanded.

That could only mean one thing: a violation. The guy was being unhelpful and unreasonable. It was my turn to be angry.

"Get stuffed," I said and hung up.

Melville looked like a deer caught in transport truck headlights.

"Pretend you didn't hear that," I said.

Later that day I told Henry about my run-in with Mr. Miserable and the new codes. At his suggestion, I called the control tower supervisor to ask for a copy of the codes in case others were different. The secretary said the supervisor was away at a meeting. She didn't know anything about codes but promised to pass on my request.

I didn't hear back from the supervisor. I got busy and forgot to call him again. The next week, The Flying Circus received a double registered letter from the Department of Transport requesting photocopies of the company daily flight sheets and aircraft log book pages for Tango Victor Hotel for the day of the flight with Melville. Obviously Mr. Miserable had followed through with the violation. The requested documents were sent. Two weeks later, I received a notice of a double registered letter in my rural mailbox. I had to take a half-day off to go to the local post office during business hours and sign for the letter.

"Dear Sir;

This is to confirm that you were the pilot of aircraft 'CF-TVH' flying in the vicinity of the Circus Airport on May 5th at 15:00 GMT.

41

At the time and in that place, the said aircraft was observed being operated in violation of the Aeronautical Act, Minimum Altitude Order by flying below 500 feet above ground off the end of Circus Airport Runway 24.

Please confirm that you were the pilot of the said aircraft at the said time and place and show cause as to why action should not be taken against you.

Sincerely,

Regional Superintendant of Air Regulation

Department of Transport"

I took the letter to the office and showed it to Henry.

"The pinch for 'low flying' is shaky," he said handing the letter back. "Low flying is allowed during training."

"That's what I thought but who wants to bat against the Department of Transport?"

"Well, are you just going to roll over and let them fine you or suspend your licence?"

"What would you do?"

"They're trying to charge you. I'd charge them," he said calmly. "It's their stupid system that broke down."

"That's big talk. How does it get me out of this violation?"

"You go flying with your next student," he said patiently. "I'll draft a letter."

When I returned from flying, Henry showed me what he had written.

"Dear Sir;

In reference to your letter of May 25.

1/ I was the pilot of the said aircraft on the said date and time and at the said place.

2/ At the time I was low flying off the end of the Circus Airport Runway 24 while executing a declared engine failure training exercise with a student pilot.

Engine failure training exercises are required by the Private Pilot training curriculum which is set by your department and is allowed under the Aeronautics Act. If this has changed, please let me know immediately. I train students every day and plan to continue to low fly during the exercises where it is required.

I would like to bring something to your attention. At The Flying

Circus, we announce the engine failure training exercises conducted near the airport through a pre-arranged code. This way the air traffic controllers know what we are doing. I am appalled to discover that these codes differ from one airport in your region to another. I do not understand how this was allowed to happen. I recently moved here from another airport and the inconsistency of the codes placed me in a situation where the Circus air traffic controller had no idea what I was doing. Fortunately no danger was created this time. It is imperative that you rectify this problem immediately. Training flights are being conducted in your region every day. As chief flying instructor of The Flying Circus, I have suspended the use of training codes by my staff at all airports until we receive notice of their standardization.

    cc: The Supervisor, Circus ATC
        Air Traffic Controller Union
        Minister of Transport"

"This is fantastic! Where did you learn to do stuff like this?" Henry just smiled and shrugged. "I'm going to enjoy working with you," I said. "I'll send this right away."

I sent the letter and never heard a thing. I did not receive a follow-up to the investigation and there was no change to the system of codes circulated. I complained about this to Henry.

"Call them up and asked what happened to your violation," he said with a laugh.

"I think I deserve a reply but I don't want to stir them up."

"I'd suggest they're counting on it," he said. "Better to let sleeping dogs lie."

Shortly after that conversation I had the opportunity to pay back the miserable air traffic controller. Melville Passmore continued taking lessons with me by starting a Night Rating. One evening we scheduled instrument flying after sunset. Melville called Circus Ground Control. Reading from his kneeboard, he asked for taxi instructions for a local flight. Mr. Miserable was working in the tower by himself. He exercised more patience with Melville than our first encounter but he still sounded like he owned the airspace and was letting us use it under duress.

It was late and there was no other air traffic in the Circus area. Melville and I took off for a local flight to the southwest. Melville called clear of the five-mile control zone but we left the radio on

43

that frequency. Several minutes later, the controller made an announcement. "All air traffic in the Circus area be advised that the control tower frequency will be unmanned for several minutes. Any aircraft requiring communications with Circus tower please advise."

There was no reply.

This could only mean one thing. Mr. Miserable had to go to the bathroom which, in the standard tower layout, was down the metal spiral staircase to the second floor. The cross-legged controller would be turning up his receiver volume and trotting downstairs.

I waited one minute. Melville was practising flying on instruments with his vision restricted by a hood. When I figured that Mr. Miserable was seated comfortably on the can with the door open and the volume upstairs turned up, I picked up our microphone, summoned my deepest, deep voice and said, "Circus tower, this is Major Airlines training flight triple three, a DC-8 heavy. Toronto is a little tied up right now and we're looking for some approach practise. Go ahead your airport advisory."

I imagined Mr. Miserable hustling up the stairs with his pants at half mast and maybe trailing toilet paper.

"Circus tower, Major triple three, do you read?" I boomed louder and deeper.

I think the timing was perfect.

"Major triple three heavy," came a breathless, squeaky reply, the winds are 200 degrees at five, altimeter 30.02, active Runway 24, we have one aircraft to the southwest, over?"

I did not reply. I nearly wet myself thinking of the controller, short of breath, leaning on the radio console with microphone in hand and pants on the floor thinking that he was about to work the first big airplane of his career.

45

Melville flew along happily trying to keep the Cherokee straight without looking outside.

"Major triple three heavy, Circus tower, do you read?"

I didn't reply.

I asked Melville to try a gentle turn.

"Foxtrot Tango Victor Hotel, Circus tower, do you read?"

I still didn't reply. I was clear of the Circus control zone and could have legitimately changed frequencies. Besides, I knew I couldn't reply with a straight face.

Chapter Seven

MOBY DAVE

"Pull back!" I bellowed into the headset.

"I am!" my student yelled.

There was no panic in his shout but there was in mine. The Lake amphibian aircraft was approaching the half-way mark on the 5,000-foot runway. We were well beyond the airplane's published rotation point.

"Pull harder!" I barked.

The handbook for the Lake said it would take off in less than 1,000 feet. The rpm and manifold pressure gauges indicated we were pulling maximum power but the flying boat was accelerating worse than a cruise ship. At 3,000 feet of runway I was about to call an abort when the nosewheel started to rise.

"Don't let it come up too high!" I yelled. I had to yell because the engine and propeller were mounted behind our heads. Their roar was transmitting through the intercom into our headsets.

The student relaxed some of his back pressure. We rolled along the runway with the nose up for another 1,000 feet. The airspeed indicator advanced like the minute hand on a clock but the main wheels finally lifted off. We were flying.

It was a mistake. The Lake struggled to five feet high and stopped climbing. It hung on the cushion of air between the wings and the ground. The end of the runway flashed by. There was a two-metre-high airport perimeter fence ahead. I reached over and selected the landing gear lever "up". I could visualize the wheels slowly retracting into the wings and the hull. The "gear up" light came on just as we scraped over the fence.

With the wheels up, the Lake gained height a few millimetres at a time. The next hurdle was a line of tall trees on the other side of a cornfield. "Start a gentle turn to the left," I bellowed. I pointed to the far corner of the field.

Turning would increase our distance to the trees. It would also give me more time to decide if I should take over and belly the flying boat into the corn or let the customer try to fly it over the trees.

My accomplice on this sudden adventure was Dave Michelin, the owner of the Lake amphibian. He had come to The Flying Circus the day before with his dog looking for a seaplane instructor. He had just purchased the Lake and needed dual instruction to satisfy his insurance requirements.

Dave was a big man. He carried his bulk as one unbroken curve from chin to ankles. He looked and waddled like a whale standing on its tail. His voice had a boom to it. We introduced ourselves.

"And this is Whiskey," Dave said nodding toward an overweight bloodhound that had followed him into our office. The dog was lying down and ignoring us completely.

"Skid Sicamore said you're an experienced float pilot and could check me out on my Lake," Dave announced in his deep voice. "He told me that he arranged it with my insurance company."

I knew Sicamore and I was immediately worried. He was a slimy aircraft salesman based in Derry. Customer satisfaction was not part of Sicamore's operation. He was right about my float flying experience but I had never flown a Lake or any other flying boat before.

"Where's the airplane now, Dave?" I asked.

"Skid's delivering it tonight," he said and then added, "after dark."

I didn't know it at the time but Dave's airplane purchase represented everything that could go wrong when an inexperienced pilot with a dream meets a slippery aircraft broker. Dave's Lake was an early model. These were underpowered and not easy to fly. The previous owner made do with the small engine by using all of its 180 horsepower all of the time. He flogged the airplane to death and then put it up for sale. The airplane sat in a field for two years before Dave asked Skid Sicamore to find him an airplane to fly to his cottage. The broker had the grime washed off the Lake and showed it to Dave. It was just what he needed to escape north on the weekends. He bought the airplane without flying it or having a mechanic check it over.

When we met, I had no reason to speculate on Dave's purchase until I saw the airplane. I didn't tell him that I had never flown one either. I wanted his business.

Dave seemed to be a likeable guy. He talked easily and laughed a lot. He told me that he worked as a relief dentist. "I fill-in for dentists who need sick leave or an extended holiday," he said. "That's fill-in, not fillin'," he laughed. "It's a good job. I get more time off than a regular dentist and I don't have to invest in an office or equipment."

While we talked, Dave drew from an endless repertoire of dental office jokes, the ones that don't require a response. It was easy to imagine Dave stuffing a patient's mouth full of hardware and then cracking a series of one-liners.

"If someone with a multiple personality disorder threatens suicide, is that considered a hostage taking?" he asked.

"I don't know," I answered politely.

"Me either," Dave said with a hearty laugh.

Between jokes, Dave told me that he had learned to fly a long time ago on an air cadet scholarship. When he received his pilot licence, he dreamed of flying a seaplane north to his parents' cottage for weekend get-a-ways. He said that he had never forgotten the dream but gave up flying to put himself through dentistry. Then he spent the next 10 years establishing a practice, paying off school debts, getting married, buying a house and, by my observation, growing jolly and fat.

Dave said that the family cottage was now his so he had bought the Lake amphibian to follow his dream. He was not currently on a job so I booked a flight with him first thing the next day.

My fears about Dave's airplane were confirmed in the morning. I arrived to find a Lake parked in the middle of our ramp. It sat dripping fuel and oil from the engine pylon. I should have cancelled the lesson as soon as I saw the aircraft's registration, "C-ADUD".

I tried to look into the cockpit through the crazed, yellowed, dirty windows. The pilot-side gull-wing door was unlocked so I opened it. The interior and instrument panel were in sad shape and out-of-date. I picked up the logbooks from the passenger seat. The only entries for the last two years were both under yesterday's date: Skid's flight and an annual maintenance inspection. I recognized the mechanic's name. He had a reputation for performing $100 annual inspections without seeing the airplane.

There was an operating handbook in one of the torn side pockets. I scooped it up, walked to the office and made some coffee. I read the operating manual until Dave arrived with a box of cream-filled donuts. "Tell me," he bellowed through a big grin, "if a turtle loses his shell, is he homeless or naked?"

The bloodhound was with him again. We poured ourselves coffee and sat down for a briefing over donuts.

One of the quirks of aviation insurance is that it automatically covers flying instructors when giving lessons to aircraft owners but instructors are not covered if they want to fly the airplane by themselves first. Special arrangements could have been made but that would have required me to admit that I didn't have any experience on that type of airplane. My first flight in the Lake was going to be a lesson with Dave.

I briefed him on what I had learned from the operating handbook. His mouth was full of donut most of the time. Occasionally he'd toss one to Whiskey who was sleeping on the floor. The dog ignored the offerings. When we finished the briefing, there was a circle of donuts littering the floor around the dog. I asked Dave if he had any questions.

"Tell me," he said with a cream-filled grin, "if a man is standing alone with no women around, is he still wrong?"

When we got up to go outside, the dog scooped the five donuts off the floor, swallowed them whole and followed us through the door.

50

"Are you going to put Whiskey in your car while we go flying?"

"Hell no," Dave replied with a laugh. "He goes where I do. If I left him in the car he'd trash it. That's how I lost my Mercedes."

"So you want to take him flying?"

"Sure, he'll be fine."

Dave and I did the pre-flight inspection together. The dentist might have been good at drilling tiny holes in teeth but mechanical or athletic he was not. The concept of standing on the Lake's oil-soaked turtle deck and opening the clamshell engine cowling was too much for him. The fact that he was wearing leather shoes and dress pants didn't help. He giggled and slid his way onto the wing and then hauled himself upright with the engine pylon. I didn't try to help him because I didn't want to be underneath when he fell. When he finally had balanced himself beside the engine, he couldn't figure how to release the latches.

"Now what do I do?" he said.

"Get down and I'll show you," I replied. "There isn't room up there for the two of us."

I completed the walkaround inspection while he watched and cracked jokes.

I didn't need to check the oil to know that it was down. Everything aft of the engine was covered with it. The airplane was also out of gas. I added oil and fuel while Dave cheered me on.

His dog was equally unathletic. When we were ready to go, Dave had to gather him up like a pile of wet laundry, stagger over to the pilot doorsill and dump him in the back seat. The fact that Dave started to giggle under the exertion made it even harder.

Dave and I climbed into the front seats. It was a tight fit. The Lake was a four-place airplane but the seats were too small for the big dentist. I turned a little sideways to give him more room.

I helped Dave through the checklist. At "engine start", he had to crank it several times before we found the right combination of mixture and power settings that would make it fire.

The Lake's instruments should have been a clue as to how the rest of the airplane would perform. Parked on the ramp with the engine idling, the airspeed indicator read 42 mph. The altimeter showed 560 feet too low when set to the current barometric reading. Since the Circus Airport was at 400 feet above sea level, this put us at an altitude of minus 160. The vertical speed indicator showed a descent that corresponded with the needle hanging straight down. The directional gyro spun left while the compass turned right. We hadn't moved yet. I turned on the transponder, ADF and VOR receivers. They didn't seem to work. The communication radio crackled to life. If it hadn't, I could have scrubbed the flight.

I called Circus Ground Control for taxi instructions. We were cleared to Runway 24.

It took us 10 minutes to taxi the Lake out to the side of the runway. Dave tried it first. The nose wheel on the airplane was fully castoring. It was steered with the left or right brake on the main wheels controlled through the top of the rudder pedals. The nose wheel had a natural tendency to flop to one side or the other. It was like trying to steer a wheelbarrow along the top of a sewer pipe. I had to get out and turn the nose away from the side of the runway twice. I tried taxiing it myself. With some experimenting, I found I could keep it on the asphalt, although drunkenly, by pressing both brakes at once and then squeezing one more than the other to steer.

I held the gull-wing door open on my side for fresh air. Whiskey rested his chin on my right shoulder and sniffed the air. From the smell of his breath, it could have been his other end.

The pre-takeoff check indicated that the engine was working okay. I had been worried about it, knowing Skid's reputation for selling junk. I knew it used oil but I decided that if Skid could make it to Circus without running it dry, then we could do a local flight and make Dave feel like he was an airplane owner.

We had launched.

Now we were inspecting corn off the end of the runway. The City of Circus stretched out beyond the row of trees ahead.

"Keep turning left!" I yelled.

We were gaining altitude slowly but only by virtue of continuous full power.

"This airplane's a pig," I yelled.

Dave was grinning but I could tell from his white knuckles that he was working hard to hold the turn. There was sweat running off his brow but he was doing a good job for someone who had not flown anything in 20 years.

The tower controller called us. "I thought you were going west, DUD?"

"We were," I replied, "but now we're going to land."

"You're cleared to land Runway 24," the controller replied. "Are you declaring an emergency?"

We had been airborne for two minutes and had not made it above 200 feet with full power. Declaring an emergency sounded like a good idea but it wouldn't make the airplane perform any better. There was no traffic in our way and the Circus Airport did not have crash/fire/rescue services on the field.

"Negative," I replied.

"We're going to land this thing, Dave," I yelled, "and find out why it won't fly."

53

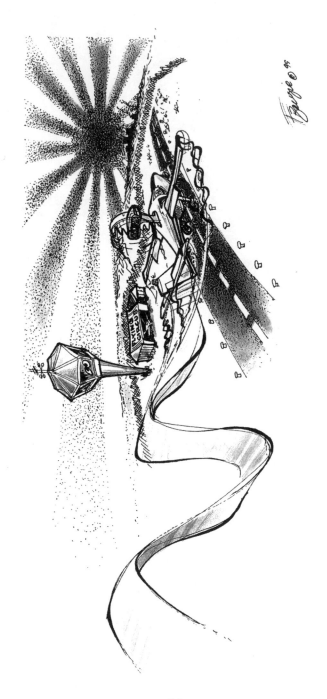

"Okay!" he yelled back. He stared intently out the windshield and hung on to the control wheel.

We turned left again to join a base leg for a landing. There was no reason to reduce the power yet. Our altitude and speed were already low. I selected the landing gear down while Dave continued flying with full power. The airplane sank. I extended half flap to see if it would create any lift. It didn't. The descent increased.

"Turn toward the runway," I yelled.

He obeyed. I continued to let Dave fly. It was easier to monitor what he was doing and what else was happening than it was to do it all myself. As we turned onto the final leg, it looked like we needed to increase our rate of descent to make the runway.

"Reduce the power," I yelled.

The next series of events started with our ignorance of the fact that the Lake amphibian reacted opposite to other aircraft during power changes. Dave reduced the power. With less thrust from the pylon over our heads, the Lake's nose pitched up. This killed some of our precious speed. The airplane started mushing toward the runway. Dave pushed the nose down. This increased the rate of descent too much. I put my hand over Dave's on the throttle and shoved it wide open again. The overhead thrust pushed the nose down further. I pulled back on the control wheel but Dave thought the nose was pitching up on its own. He pushed forward. He was stronger. The descent turned into a dive.

"I have control!" I yelled.

Dave didn't let go right away. We were going to crash nose first into the runway. I still had my hand over Dave's on the throttle. In desperation, I jerked it all the way back. This made the Lake's nose pop up suddenly. The airplane hovered over the runway for a split second, the airspeed died and we plopped gently onto the asphalt.

Dave let go of everything. I squeezed the brakes with my toes and turned off the runway.

Dave's eyes were wide and the sweat was running hard.

"Now I know why Kamikaze pilots wore helmets," he said.

Chapter Eight

WIRED

On Thursday morning, four Provincial Hydro service trucks pulled into The Flying Circus parking lot. Henry was flying with Moose. I was in the office making up an advertisement for the newspaper "Personal" column.

The trucks were monster linemen vehicles, the kind that would stir the heart of any four-year-old boy. They were loaded with rope and wire spools and rimmed with built-in compartments. Two of them had crew cabs forward and cherry pickers aft. The other two were stopped nose-to-tail on the entrance road. The last one was pulling a backhoe rig on a trailer. About ten men dressed in various levels of orange overalls, boots, gauntlets, DayGlo vests and hard-hats descended from the cabs. They stood by looking at the air-planes and the buildings.

I recognized Bruce Stanwick in a white hardhat. He pulled a large metal cone from the back of one truck and started walking toward the office. I went outside to greet him.

"Hi, Bruce. Did you bring all these guys for flying lessons?" I asked with a laugh.

"Not today," Bruce answered with his usual thin smile. "We had some of these kicking around the yard," he said, lifting the cone toward me. "I thought maybe they might be okay for your hangar."

The cone had a glass globe inside.

"What is it?" I asked.

"A mercury vapor light," he replied.

"I don't know anything about them, Bruce," I said, "but I do know that we don't have the money for things like that right now."

Bruce maintained his smile. "They're used. We took them off some government buildings that were being upgraded. They'll last a long time yet but to the hydro company they're scrap. You can have them if you want. They're 1,000 watts each. Four of them ought to light up that hangar fairly well."

"That's really generous of you, Bruce," I said. I felt awkward. I had only flown with Bruce twice and he had said very little. I didn't feel like I knew him at all but I didn't want to turn away a gift horse.

"Sure, we'll take them," I said. "Thank you very much." I reached to take the light from his hand. "I'll help you unload them. We can store them in the back of the hangar for now. We'll have them put up when we can afford it." Then I added, "If you've got time, I'll make your boys some coffee."

"No thanks," Bruce said. He hung onto the light and waved to the crew with his free hand. "We just came from the donut shop." Then his smile broadened, "I've tried your coffee."

One of the men started the backhoe while two others flipped down the trailer ramps. The rest of the crew started unloading wire and lights from the trucks. I gave Bruce a puzzled look.

"You don't have any power to the hangar yet," he explained. "We've got a few minutes before our next job so we'll run a line underground from that pole over there. We have some wire and a panel left over from another job so we'll rig the lights for you."

"We can't afford it right now, Bruce," I said with more emphasis.

"I understand," Bruce replied. "You're just starting out. That's why we're here. We're helping." He spoke the last two words slowly, almost spelling them out. "This won't cost you anything, trust me."

"I don't know what to say," I said.

"Don't say anything. Just pull the airplane out of the hangar so we can drive the cherry pickers in."

"Okay, Bruce."

It took them about forty minutes. One crew dug a slit trench from the nearest pole to the hangar, laid wire and filled it in. While they were at it, they ran wires to the fuel tanks.

"I know where I can get you a couple of used electric fuel pumps for those tanks," Bruce explained.

Two other crews drove their cherry picker trucks into the hangar. They hung two lights each on the steel rafters. A fourth crew rigged an electrical service panel in the corner of the hangar.

I stood with my mouth open for a while and then got busy. I made two pots of coffee with full measures of grounds for each. Then I hand wrote ten gift certificates for sightseeing flights. When the crews were packing up, I went out and spoke to Bruce. "I made

57

coffee with fresh grounds and a full scoop per cup. Do your guys have time?"

"Sure," he said with a grin. He waved the men toward the office.

When they were all inside, there was a pile of muddy boots at the door and the portable classroom was wall-to-wall bodies in orange coveralls. They helped themselves to the coffee while I passed out the gift certificates.

"We don't have any fancy letterhead yet," I explained, "but these are good for a free flight. You can either use it for an introductory flying lesson or bring a friend or family member for a sightseeing flight over the area."

"Give George two," one of the men said with a laugh, "he's afraid of heights."

"Do people get sick when the're flying?" one of the men asked.

"They do if they're not in an airplane," another guy joked.

"They fly you upside down," still another worker said, "so you don't know which way to throw up."

"If you'd rather not use the certificate," I offered, "give it to a friend but ask them to call ahead to book the flight. Is there anyone who wants to arrange something while you're here?"

Several of the men scheduled sightseeing flights for the coming weekend.

"Are you sure you don't want to come out during the week?" I asked. "The weather is supposed to be good tomorrow."

Most of them chuckled at this suggestion. "Hell no, we have to work tomorrow," one of them said. "We never goof off during company time."

They all laughed.

"Well, I really appreciate what you've done for us today," I said. "This company would have been in the dark for a long time if you hadn't come along."

Within a couple of minutes, the men downed their coffee, placed their cups in the garbage and started out the door as if there had been a signal from Bruce. I hadn't seen any.

At the end of the day, Henry and I were finished around sunset.

"I'll get my car," I said. It was our standard procedure to light up the hangar with our headlights when we put the airplanes away at night.

"Okay, I'll meet you out there," he replied.

On the way to the parking lot, I switched on the new hangar

lights. I drove my Volkswagen Beetle around to the ramp and pointed it toward the hangar opening with its lights off. The glow from the mercury vapor lights flooded the hangar and spilled onto the ramp.

Henry came out of the office and we pulled the first Cherokee toward the hangar.

"Isn't it great this time of year when it stays lighter later?" he asked.

"Yes," I replied.

He looked at the horizon where the sun had gone down. It was black. He looked in the hangar, looked at the lightless Volkswagon and then looked up.

"Where did they come from?"

"Bruce Stanwick dropped by with a few workmen and put them up this morning."

"You're kidding."

"I'm not kidding."

"What did that cost?"

"Sightseeing flights for ten hydro linemen."

"You're kidding."

"I'm not kidding."

"What's the catch?"

"You have to do the flights on your day off this weekend."

Chapter Nine

HIRED

On Friday, Barry McDay walked into The Flying Circus office and introduced himself. I recognized his voice. He was an air traffic controller from the local tower. Barry appeared to be young, lean and bright. He stood erect and the intensity in his eyes indicated that his lights were on and someone was home.

He explained to Henry and me that he had obtained a Commercial Pilot Licence at the last airport where he had worked before moving to Circus.

"I'd like to get a Flight Instructor Rating and teach part time," he announced.

I immediately thought that we needed customers, not staff.

"Good," Henry replied. "Both of us are qualified to teach instructors."

"If I took my training here," Barry asked, "would you guarantee me a part-time teaching job?"

"No," I thought to myself.

"Yes," Henry answered quickly. "In fact, I'll hire you right now if you'll agree to certain terms. Would you like a coffee?"

"Yes, sir, I would."

I wanted to take Henry out behind the hangar and talk sense into him. The few customers that we had were not enough to pay all the bills let alone put food on the table. If we started hiring staff and acting like managers, we'd be broke faster than we were going broke now. I didn't say anything immediately. I had learned in the last week that Henry and I did not think the same. He was smarter.

"First of all," Henry said, "don't call me 'Sir'."

"Okay, Henry," Barry replied. He smiled and relaxed slightly.

"You start working tomorrow. We have a dozen sightseeing flights and introductory flying lessons booked over Saturday and Sunday. These are promotional flights for some Provincial Hydro workers so we can't pay you for them but we'll credit you with free flying time on the airplanes. These flights will count on your instructor's course, which will save you money."

"I'm working afternoons this weekend," Barry said. "I won't be able to fly after two thirty."

"That's okay. We'll do the later flights. While you're on the instructor course, you'll teach ground school in the evenings that you're available and continue to do introductory flying lessons and sightseeing flights for credit. You'll be expected to develop your own student customers by the time you graduate. We'll supply you with brochures and the occasional low-budget newspaper advertisement."

"Agreed," Barry said.

"When you're on course," Henry continued, "you might be bumped off a lesson or two in favor of a paying customer. If this or anything else becomes a problem, you speak to either my partner or me. If you're a problem for us, we'll speak to you."

"Agreed."

"Finally, all of the above is dependant on my partner flying with you right now. If he doesn't like how you fly, the deal is off. I'll need to see your pilot licence and medical certificate. I'd also like two work references other than the control tower supervisor or your mother. Any questions?"

"Just one," Barry said looking into his cup. "Who makes the coffee around here?"

"When you're working here, you do," Henry said, holding out his right hand, "Do we have a deal?"

"Yes sir, I mean Henry," Barry said. He handed Henry an envelope that he dug from his pocket. "The references are in here."

He turned to me and shook my hand. "I appreciate the opportunity to show what I can do," he said to me. "I'll just go out to my car and fetch my sunglasses and checklist. I'll be right back."

As soon as he had cleared the door, Henry turned immediately to me. He had a worried look on his face. "Did I go too far? Is everything I said okay with you? We can still cancel the agreement. We don't have anything in writing."

"No," I said, "I think you covered everything quite well. We'll give him a try. If he's as sharp as he looks, we should be all right. There is just one thing that bothers me."

"What's that?" he asked quickly.

"The references are in here."

"It's scary how much you sounded like our former boss, Stingy Mingy."

"Damn," Henry said shaking his head. "You're right."

63

Chapter Ten

"TEN-FOUR BIG BUDDY"

"What would you like to do?" Barry McDay asked as we walked to the hangar for his interview flight.

"Show me how you'd conduct an introductory flying lesson," I replied.

During the pre-flight inspection, he treated me like a prospective customer. He explained a few things, asked some easy questions and involved me in a couple of items such as checking the oil. I was pleasantly surprised. Barry had no training or experience as a flying instructor. I felt good about hiring him before we had climbed into the airplane.

Barry offered me the left seat. He went through the start check explaining a few of the basics. He started the engine, turned on the radio, picked up the microphone and handed it to me.

"Can you get us taxi instructions for a local flight?" he asked. He was blushing.

"No," I replied, handing the microphone back. "This is my first time in a small airplane and microphones scare me to death."

His face turned completely red. "I don't really want the other guys in the control tower to know I'm doing this," he said shyly.

I didn't budge.

"None of the controllers in this tower have a pilot's licence," he explained. "They're overly sensitive to any suggestion that they need to fly to be good air traffic controllers."

"I'm heartbroken," I said sarcastically.

Barry's face turned redder. "They don't know that I'm a pilot," he confessed.

"I see," I said. It wasn't a big deal to me so I took the microphone and called the ground controller for taxi instructions.

The rest of our airborne interview went well. He sold me on the idea that learning to fly would be fun and that he was a good find for The Flying Circus. I showed him our special procedures for sightseeing flights over nearby Niagara Falls.

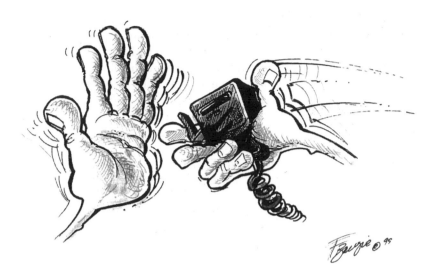

"I don't really want the other guys in the control tower to know I'm doing this," he said shyly.

Back in the office, I asked him how many air traffic controllers worked in the tower.

"Nine, counting the supervisor," he replied.

"If I give you eight introductory flying lesson gift certificates, would you pass them around at work? Maybe we can change the 100 per cent non-flying ratio in the tower."

He held up his palm. "Don't rush it. The 'no flying' thing is like a glue holding this group together. That's why I have never mentioned my pilot licence."

"Okay," I said, "but they're welcome to fly here any time."

That weekend our phone rang off the hook. Leanne's idea of placing an ad in the "Personal" column worked really well. The weather was great and the newspaper advertising generated a steady stream of introductory flying lesson customers. Barry flew the wings off the Cherokees. Henry and I kept him going from one customer to another. We took turns flying the other airplane and

65

working the flight desk. The office was busy with prospective students and the hydro workers who came in for sightseeing flights.

Barry seemed to enjoy the activity but we had a radio monitor in the office and I never heard him speak to the control tower. Instead, the air traffic controllers were treated to a series of halting requests for taxi, takeoff and landing instructions. Occasionally the first-time students would hold the microphone button down and you could hear Barry in the background telling them what to say. The hydro workers were the best.

"Got your ears on big buddy?" they boomed into the microphone. "This is Tango Victor Hotel. We wanna take this rig to see Niagara Falls."

The microphone would click off and then back on. "Come on?"

Each time the controller finished giving them instructions, they'd answer, "Ten-four, big buddy."

Chapter Eleven

LEANNE

By the end of our second week in business, Henry and I felt great. The newspaper advertising brought us new students and Barry had proven to be a great find. He willingly helped with cleaning and fueling the airplanes. He volunteered time in the office to answer the telephone and was a hit with the customers.

After work on the Monday, Henry and I bought Barry a beer at the local pub. It had been another good flying day. It was nine o'clock by the time we had put the airplanes away. We should have been going home to our families but we felt we owed the beer to Barry and ourselves.

"I left you a note in the cash box," Barry said when we were sitting in the bar. "One of the phone calls today was from the fuel company wondering when they might get paid for the avgas."

Henry and I looked at each other knowingly. Part of our business plan had been to maintain the company books every night before going home. Fifteen days later, we had not made a single accounting entry. Henry had been making bank deposits in the evening but we had no idea how much money had come in. I had been picking up the mail and placing it in a drawer unopened. We had not paid any bills.

"Maybe I'll ask Leanne to come in for a few hours tomorrow," Henry offered. "She can open the mail and pay a few bills. Is that all right with you?"

"Sure," I replied, sipping a beer. "Does she know anything about accounting?"

"She can balance a cheque book."

"That's good enough for me."

Leanne had spent the last eight years trapped at home with two kids and eight years before that teaching primary grades in school. They were not very good clerical qualifications but if she was willing to help for a day to get our paperwork on track, I had no objection.

I was already in the office when Leanne and Henry arrived the next morning. Her hair was short and she was wearing a big dress with one of Henry's old baseball jackets over top. She looked like a schoolteacher. She walked and stood with her feet apart as if to defy any eight year old to knock her over.

"Welcome to The Flying Circus, Leanne," I said with a smile. "I appreciate your coming. Would you like a cup of coffee?"

"Yes, thank you very much," she said.

She gave the office a slow, once-over look. If she was nervous about helping us, it didn't show. I poured the coffee and she fixed it up with double cream and sugar.

"Could you spend a few minutes showing me what needs to be done?" she asked. "I think that'll work better than Henry telling me." She talked like a primary school teacher, s-l-o-w-l-y and c-l-e-a-r-l-y.

"Sure, Leanne. Bring your coffee behind the desk."

I showed her the drawer crammed with unopened mail, the cash box, the bank deposit slips, the unopened accounting ledger and our unused cheque book.

"If you could open the mail and pay some bills, that would be a great help," I said. "We eventually need to set up some system of accounting."

I also asked her to answer the telephone when Henry and I were both flying and to take messages.

She asked one question. "Do we lose customers over this terrible coffee?"

"Two dead and three wounded," Henry answered quickly.

"I used yesterday's grounds," I confessed.

Leanne took the pot to the bathroom in the corner of the office, dumped it and brought back fresh water. She dug in the cupboard under the coffee maker and pulled out a fresh bag of coffee.

Barry walked in. He was my first student of the day.

"Leanne," Henry said, "this is Barry McDay, the fellow who helps us out while working on his Instructor's Rating."

Leanne covered the length of the office in three wide strides.

"Pleased to meet you Barry," she said, giving his arm a few good pumps.

"I'm pleased to meet you, Mrs. Rains," he replied.

"Leanne," Henry corrected.

"Leanne," Barry said.

"Is your mother Scottish as well?" Leanne asked. It was a nosey schoolteacher question delivered from out of nowhere.

Barry hesitated but he had the right answer. "Both my parents are Canadian."

Leanne wasn't put off that easily. "Where does your red hair come from?" she asked. She obviously was a woman who had been cooped up too long.

Barry responded before Henry and I could rescue him. "Actually," Barry said, "my great, great, great grandmother was raped by a band of roving Vikings."

I had a mouthful of coffee and nearly choked on it. It was a perfect response to an inappropriate question. Henry rocked on his heels with laughter.

"What's so funny?" Leanne asked. "Barry, you should be proud of your mixed heritage." She sounded like she genuinely believed him.

Henry and I managed to stop laughing, but we couldn't get the smirks off our faces.

"Yes, ma'am," Barry replied with a smile, "I am."

I bailed Barry out of any further probing by starting our instructor lesson. We did a ground briefing while Henry pulled the airplanes out. Leanne opened the mail, sorting it into neat piles.

When Barry and I returned from our flight, Leanne was busy grilling Margaret Hathaway, my next student, about her background. I was worried that Leanne's probing would bother the customers but it sounded like Margaret was happily responding with full details. When I finished with Barry, I had to interrupt them to take Margaret flying.

When we came back down, Leanne was sparring with Al Milton from behind the flight desk. Al was leaning on the counter and sparring right back.

"How did you get roped into working for these two losers?" Al asked in a loud voice as I walked into the office. It was obvious that the line, delivered with a chuckle, was for my benefit.

"I'm married to Henry," Leanne replied.

"Oh no!" Al exclaimed and laughed. "Here I was beginning to think you were an intelligent woman."

"Thank you," Leanne replied without hesitation. "I said we were married. I didn't say I was taking flying lessons from him."

Lucky for Leanne, Al could take it as well as give it. He laughed

69

so hard that he spilled his coffee on the floor.

"Careful there," Leanne said, "I just washed that floor." She handed Al a paper towel.

I looked down. She had indeed cleaned the floor. She had also rearranged the furniture. We now had a distinct office area, a teaching area in front of the blackboard and a lounge area around the coffee pot. It looked like she was taking over.

"These guys must pay you a lot to put up with them," Al said. He was obviously trying to keep the sarcasm flowing.

"They can't afford it," Leanne replied as she handed me Margaret's invoice. It was filled out in perfect teacher printing.

Before Al could say anything else, Leanne turned to him and said, "But I get to sleep with one of the managing partners."

Al had to cover his mouth to keep from spewing more coffee. "Well that's got to be worth 50 cents," he chuckled after swallowing.

Henry walked through the door.

Al pointed to Leanne. "You should put a leash on this women," he said with a laugh. "She's telling everyone about her sex life."

Henry's eyes popped at the comment. He was not aware of the familiarity that Leanne had so quickly developed with Al.

"I only told him that I was working for trade rather than money," Leanne said.

I wondered if the conversation might be a too racy for Margaret but she laughed harder than anyone at the last comment.

Margaret signed her bill and booked another couple of lessons. Henry started a ground briefing with Al. Margaret left and Henry and Al went flying.

"Can I show you what I've done with the booking sheets?" Leanne asked me.

She had color-coded the lesson schedule with different marker pens for Henry, Barry and me.

"We received three calls from the newspaper ad about learning to fly," she said. "I scheduled introductory lessons for them with Barry."

"That's good," I said.

"Melville Passmore called," she continued. "He cancelled tonight's lesson with you so I booked it on Thursday."

"Okay, thank you," I said. "I appreciate what you're doing."

Leanne was obviously digging in. It looked like she was planning to work for more than one day. I had mixed feelings about that. It was nice to have her help but I wasn't sure about my partner's

"It's the fuel dealer," she said.

wife working in the office permanently.

"I'm enjoying myself," she said. "It's fun to work with adults for a change."

"Well, we'll pay you for your time," I said, adding an element of closure to the situation.

"You can't afford it," she replied frankly. She looked at me and smiled. "Not yet anyway. I've been through the deposits and bills. Business has been good but you're still playing catch-up with your start-up costs. This school is going to need more than shoebox

71

accounting. I took the liberty to make an appointment with an accountant in town tomorrow. He can start me on one of those one-write bookkeeping systems."

She sounded like she was making a permanent job for herself. The telephone rang before I could say anything. Leanne picked it up without hesitation.

"Good afternoon, The Flying Circus," she said crisply. She listened to the person on the other end of the line without looking at me. "I handle the company's bookkeeping, you can talk to me."

I tried to catch her attention to see if I could help.

"We couldn't possibly pay that now," she said into the telephone. Her voice sounded neither worried nor apologetic. "I went over the bank statements today and we don't have that kind of money."

It was obviously an irate supplier. I wanted to know who she was talking to. I leaned over and caught her eye. She covered the mouthpiece.

"It's the fuel dealer," she said. Before I could say anything, she looked the other way. "I'll send you something now and then some more next week," she offered to the person on the phone. "I'll make sure we're paid up before we order more fuel." She was sounding very confident.

"My name is Leanne Rains. Call me anytime," she said.

"Well thank you. Good bye."

"I don't mind helping out," Leanne said to me as if there had been no irate telephone call, "but it's your business. I expect you to tell me if I'm out of line."

"It's our business, Leanne," I said extending my hand. "Welcome to The Flying Circus."

Chapter Twelve

DEAD WHALES DON'T FLY

" She's toast."

The voice at on the other end of the line belonged to Darcy Philips. Darcy was the chief mechanic at our former employer, Derry Air. Our contract to lease two Piper Cherokees from Derry Air also made him the chief mechanic for The Flying Circus.

"What's toast, Darcy?" I asked.

"The whale."

I had arranged for Darcy's shop to check over Dave Michelin's Lake amphibian to see what it needed. Darcy had come to Circus and flown it back to Derry.

"What's wrong with it, Darcy?"

"It's toast."

Darcy never wasted a full sentence on pilots. He regarded us as idiots. It was a logical conclusion drawn by a man who spent all day fixing airplanes broken by pilots.

"Is the engine bad?"

"Scrap."

"The instruments?"

"History."

"The radios?"

"Dead."

"But the communication radio worked when I flew it."

"Not any more and there's nobody old enough to fix it."

"Anything else?"

"Everything else."

"How about the hydraulics, fuel system, electrics and the airframe?"

"Leaking, leaking, cooked and rotten."

"Can we go a little slower so I can explain this to the customer?"

"Your customer's an idiot."

"What's wrong with the engine?"

"Broken rings for starters. There's more compression in a nine-

73

ty-year-old hooker."

"The instruments?"

"All out of limits except the clock."

"The electrics?"

"The hydraulics and fuel systems are leaking into the hull. It's a race to see if the fluid corrodes the bottom out of the airplane before the half-baked electric system sets fire to the whole thing."

"Can't it be fixed?"

"Fix is a function of wallet. How fat is your whale lover?"

"What's the bottom line?"

"Twenty-five thousand dollars."

"That's more than it's worth!"

"You asked."

"I'll call you back."

"Fix it," Dave boomed.

I phoned Dave Michelin and suggested that he stop by the office to discuss the repair quote on his airplane. When I came in from my next flight, he was eating jelly donuts on the couch and tossing one-liners across the office to Leanne. His hound was flopped on the floor.

"Did you ever wonder why the Psychic Hotline asks your name?" Dave asked Leanne.

"No, why?" Leanne replied.

"Beats me."

I finished with my student and pulled a chair up beside Dave. The couch was already full. He waved a donut at me. "Help yourself," he said with a hearty laugh. There was a ring of icing sugar around his mouth. "They're recommended by four out of five dentists."

"I hate to spoil your day, Dave," I said, "but Darcy estimates it'll cost $25,000 to fix the Lake."

"Go for it," he said without hesitation.

It took a moment for what he said to sink in. "Before you make any hasty decisions, let me find out the scrap value of the airplane," I suggested. "You'd get some of your money back."

"Fix it," Dave boomed.

"If you pay the $25,000, you'll still have an old Lake worth little more than you paid for it."

"If I sell it for scrap, then I lose my money and I don't have an airplane. Tell your man to do the repairs and then I want new windows, paint and interior. I'll go to $35,000. That way I'll salvage my investment and have the airplane that I want."

I didn't follow his logic but I didn't know how else I could reason with him.

"It'll take a couple of months," I said.

"It's only spring. I'll fly your Cherokees in the meantime. When can I get checked out?"

"Right now," Leanne offered. She had been listening to the conversation.

"Okay," Dave said, heaving himself up from the couch. "I'll hit the washroom and we'll go."

Dave headed for the bathroom in the corner of the office. Whiskey went with him.

"He isn't making sense," I said to Leanne when he had closed the door.

"It makes sense to me," she replied. "It's shopping logic. If you don't buy something then the money that you would have saved on the purchase is lost and you have no merchandise to show for it. In Dave's case, he has to spend more money to save losing the money that he already spent. I understand his logic perfectly but I still don't know why the Psychic Hotline asks for your name."

"Think about it," I replied.

Dave came out of the washroom. I could hear Whiskey drinking out of the bowl.

"If the seat cushion on an airliner is your personal floatation device in the event of a ditching, is the bag of peanuts your life raft?"

The three of us went flying in a Cherokee. The airplane was smaller with Dave and Whiskey in it. The dog filled both jump seats in the back. We used extra runway to takeoff. Once we were airborne, the climb rate was lower than normal. The engine seemed to be developing full power and Dave was holding the best rate of climb speed. I chalked it up to the warm temperatures that day.

Dave displayed the same natural touch with the Cherokee that he had on our short flight in the Lake but the airplane wouldn't hold altitude during level turns at 2300 rpm.

"Try 2400," I said.

The extra power helped but the performance was still sluggish. In straight flight, the Cherokee flew left wing low.

"How much do you weigh, Dave?"

He looked at me sideways. "Why do you ask?"

"Because you either weigh more than you look or there's something wrong with this airplane."

"Two thirty-five, thirty-six," he replied. "Maybe the landing gear won't retract," he added, stabbing at an imaginary lever on the dashboard.

"The landing gear's bolted down," I replied. "Is that 236 pounds or kilograms?"

"Does it matter?"

"Lots!"

Chapter Thirteen

LESSON FROM MELVILLE

Iflew most of the instrument lessons for Melville Passmore's Night Rating Course during the daylight to reduce the number of late night summer working days. On one of these lessons, we were pre-flighting the airplane together when Melville said, "I was lookin' at an airplane." The comment came from nowhere. No explanation followed. He was beating around the bush like a true farmer.

"Oh?" I said.

"I've been saving my money."

"Looking as in 'looking to buy'?" I asked.

"The farm's big enough for a landing strip."

"What kind of airplane, Melville?"

"TriPacer," he said. He glanced at me sideways.

"They're rugged," I replied. It was true.

"There's one for sale at Derry," he offered.

"At Derry Air?"

He nodded without answering. It was like he was afraid of my reaction and wanted to be able to change his mind. He had good reason. I knew the TriPacer for sale at Derry Air. It was the world's ugliest airplane. The previous owner had been involved in a near mid-air collision. After that flight he had the airplane repainted in bright yellow with red diagonal stripes. It looked like a school bus that had been sunburned through venetian blinds. The registration, C-LOWN, topped off the aircraft's laughing-stock image.

The TriPacer had been parked in the tie-down area at the back of the Derry Air ramp for over a year. It sat dirt-streaked and lopsided with a faded "For Sale" sign hanging on its propeller. The same aircraft salesman that sold Dave Michelin his Lake owned the airplane.

"Skid Sicamore owns that airplane, Melville. He has a bad reputation," I said. "I don't think you should be dealing with him."

77

"I know. I've already talked to him," Melville said. He blushed and looked down. He scuffed the floor with his work boot.

"What happened?" I asked.

"He told me to get lost."

I could picture it. The grubby little farm boy approaches the big-time aircraft salesman. Melville probably has the price of the airplane saved in cash but Skid takes one look at him and tells him to take a hike.

"Melville, let me talk to Darcy. There could be a lot of hidden things wrong with that airplane. I'll see if he knows anything about the mechanical condition."

"Can you talk to him now?" he asked shyly.

It was obvious that Melville was bitten badly by the airplane bug.

78

"We could fly to Derry today," he continued. "You could teach me instrument flyin' on the way. We could talk to Darcy, see the TriPacer and fly back."

He was having trouble suppressing the excitement in his voice.

"I'll call and see if he's there."

"I did," Melville offered. "He's there. I called before I left home."

"Okay," I said with a shrug, "let's go."

The lesson on the way to Derry was a good example of why it was always interesting to teach Melville. He was a good pilot. He handled the Cherokee with the light touch of a machinery operator. He understood the airplane mechanics and systems better than me but his brain seized when faced with traditional mathematics. Academically, Melville was slow but he was country smart. He couldn't read a shop manual but he could field-strip and repair a Ford 8N tractor in the dark. Our first lessons at Derry Air together had dragged on until I learned to stop teaching him the traditional piloting theory. Melville learned by figuring things out for himself.

Our lesson on the way to Derry was an introduction to instrument flying with a limited panel. Melville flew the Cherokee with a hood restricting his vision. I covered the attitude indicator and heading indicator with suction cup soap dishes to simulate instrument failures. Melville flew on the remaining instruments without difficulty until he needed to establish a new heading. The compass was unreliable in a turn. The trick was to set the airplane at a bank angle that gave a turn of three degrees per second on the turn coordinator, figure the number of degrees of the turn, divide it by three and turn for that many seconds.

I knew this wouldn't work for Melville so I just explained that the compass didn't work in turns. In the air, he changed heading by turning, straightening out, checking the compass and making a correction. It was a crude method at first, but by the time we reached Derry, Melville had caught the turning rhythm of a fixed bank angle. He knew how long it would take him to complete any turn without using mathematics. He could nail a new heading within five degrees.

We landed and taxied to the Derry Air ramp. Melville ran over to the TriPacer and peered through the pilot's side window.

"What do you think?" he asked excitedly.

The airplane looked worse than I remembered. The layer of dirt covering it was deeper and the tires were flatter.

"Let's talk to Darcy," I said.

I used all the body language I could muster.

We went into the Derry Air shop.

"Well if it isn't Tweedle Dee and Tweedle Dum," Darcy said. "What did you guys break today?"

"Nothing," I replied. "Melville is interested in buying Sicamore's TriPacer. We came to see if the horse's mouth could offer any advice on the airplane."

I was using all the body language I could muster: raised eyebrows, cocked head, crooked grin, winks and a big shrug. I was trying to indicate to Darcy that a sarcastic negative answer was welcome. I wanted the Derry Air mechanic to talk straight with Melville and tell him exactly what he thought of the airplane. I hoped that would be the end of it.

"The electric zebra? How much does he want for it now?" Darcy asked. He directed the question to Melville.

"Ten thousand," Melville replied.

"Offer him five," Darcy said.

I jumped right in. "Darcy, if the airplane is only worth five thousand dollars, wouldn't Melville be better off looking for another one?" I nodded my head up and down in a big affirmative motion.

"At five thousand, it's a dynamite buy," Darcy replied. "I maintained that airplane for the former owner. We recovered it before the paint shop laid the clown job on it. It was kept in good shape but when the guy wanted to move up he couldn't sell it. Skid gave him next to nothing for it as a trade-in. Offer him five thousand, Melville, and settle for six. Nobody else is going to buy it."

"But its been sitting there for over a year," I pleaded. "There could be all kinds of things wrong with it."

Darcy ignored me. "Melville, it needs tires and an inspection but I've run the engine regularly. I'll have you flying for less than $500," he said and then laughed. "And you'll never have to worry about a mid-air collision."

"Is Mr. Sicamore here?" Melville asked excitedly. Before Darcy could answer, he pulled out a roll of money that would have choked an elephant.

"He's in the lounge," Darcy said. "Go get him, tiger."

"Wait a minute, wait a minute!" I yelled. I covered the monster roll of money with my hand. "If you two guys are so stuck on this airplane, let me talk to Skid first."

Melville was leaning toward the lounge. He looked like he was ready to hand Skid ten thousand in a roll of cash.

"Before you start waving money," I said, "let me see what I can negotiate with Sicamore."

Melville frowned at the delay. I held up my hand forcefully. "I'll just be a minute. You stay here!"

I found Sicamore inside the flying school office leaning against the flight desk, talking on the telephone. He looked like a sleazy aircraft salesman. His balding pointed head and skinny neck stuck out of his wrinkled trench coat. I indicated that I wanted to talk to him. He looked the other way.

I waited close by until he was done.

81

"Hi there," he said. "I'm in a bit of a hurry, here."

Sicamore could tell when you wanted something from him.

"I have a customer interested in your TriPacer," I said.

"Great, send him around," Skid said and moved to leave.

"I'd like to establish a finder's fee," I said. "I can see this situation coming up more than once." I intended to pass whatever fee I could negotiate on to Melville. It was my way of getting the price down.

Sicamore touched my shoulder and continued to move away. "Good idea," he said. "If I sell anything to your guys, it's fifty bucks in your pocket, guaranteed."

"Five per cent," I said.

He stopped moving for a moment, thrust his hands into his trench coat pockets and looked at the floor. "Let me give you a quick lesson on aircraft sales," he said firmly. "I'm lucky if I make five per cent and you want me to do all the work, take all the risk and give you all my profit? No thanks." He turned again.

"I have a customer here now," I said quickly. "He wants that TriPacer. He loves that TriPacer and is willing to pay cash. I'm not going to introduce him to you for fifty dollars."

That stopped him.

"One hundred bucks," he said.

"We're getting closer," I replied. "Five per cent."

"One fifty. It's my final offer."

"Five per cent or we go look for another TriPacer."

"He's here now?"

"Yes."

"Okay, hotshot. Four per cent, if and only if he buys that airplane today."

"Deal," I said and stuck out my hand.

He gave it a quick pump. "Where is he?"

"Talking to Darcy."

Sicamore rolled his eyes. "Well you get him away from that jerk and I'll meet you at the tie-downs."

I felt better. At least I could give Melville the commission back but I wasn't finished. I was prepared to continue my hard-nosed negotiations for the shy farm boy. I went back into the hangar.

"Darcy, where's Melville?"

"Outside. He wants that airplane so bad he can taste it."

"How much money do you have, kid?"

I hotfooted through the hangar door and headed for the tie-down area. I was in time to see Skid shaking hands with Melville beside the TriPacer. When I was within earshot, I could hear Skid say, "Deals like this don't come around very often, sonny. This is the perfect airplane for a young fella like you."

"I see you two have met," I said as I jogged up to them.

They ignored me. Melville stood with his hands in his pockets scuffing the ground with his boot. Skid was animated. He waved his arms at the TriPacer.

"Yup, she's a beauty. Ten thousand and she's yours. Of course," he said with a chuckle, "that includes air in the tires."

I was about to tell Skid that Melville would give him five thousand dollars when the farm boy pulled a stubby hand from his pocket. He was holding the monster roll of cash. Sicamore started to lick his lips. He lifted his arm to take the money but Melville held it back.

83

"Mr. Sicamore, I'll give you $5,000 cash for that airplane right now."

Skid used his extended arm to wave him off. "Not a chance," he said and turned as if to walk away.

Melville peeled five one hundred-dollar bills off the roll and put them in his pocket. He held the remaining cash out to Sicamore. "Four thousand five hundred," he said calmly.

Skid shot me a dirty look. "Look son," he said to Melville, "if you're serious about buying this airplane, I'd like to see you own it. Now I'm willing to come down a little. Nine thousand. It's a good price and it's my final offer."

Melville peeled off five hundred more dollars and put them away. "Four thousand," he said, holding it out to Skid.

"No, I can't do it."

Melville put all the money in his pocket. "There are two other TriPacers for sale not far away," he said. "I'll look at them." He turned as if to walk away.

"Look," Skid said, touching Melville's arm, "you seem like a nice young fellow. Eight thousand five hundred and I'll include a free Certificate of Airworthiness annual inspection."

Melville pulled out the roll of bills and held it out. "I'll get my own mechanic to do the inspection, thank you. Four thousand."

"Save your money," Skid said sarcastically. "Come back and see me when you can afford the whole airplane." Skid sounded exasperated. He started to walk away. Melville looked at the ground but he didn't move. Skid made it half way to the fence. He came back.

"Talk some sense into this kid, will you?" he said to me. "I'll go as low as eight thousand dollars, as is, where is. You can't buy an airplane, any airplane for eight thousand dollars. Take it or leave it!"

"You're right, Skid," I said, "it's a good price for most airplanes but this isn't most airplanes. Look at it. Melville's doing you a big favor."

Skid turned to the young farmer. "Seventy-five hundred; have you got seven thousand five hundred kid?"

I was enjoying this. The shy farmer was getting the better of the sly salesman and we all knew it. Melville pulled the roll of bills from his pocket. "Four thousand," he said.

"Forget it," Skid said. He spun around in his tracks and stomped away.

I was proud of Melville for letting the deal go at $7,500. I knew that if he bought it, I would be flying with him. I didn't relish the comments on the radio that it would solicit. We could find another TriPacer.

Melville didn't move. We stood beside the airplane saying nothing. Skid made it through the fence gate and half way to his car. He stopped and turned. He put his hands on his hips and then marched back with his trench coat flapping behind him. He went straight to Melville.

"How much money do you really have, kid?"

Melville pulled out the same roll. He held it out to Skid. "Four thousand," he said.

"Come on," Skid said pointing to the other pocket. "How much all together?"

Melville reached into his other front pocket. "Five thousand."

"It's not enough," Skid said but his hand was hovering. "You'll have to do better than that."

"How much better?" Melville asked. He kept his voice low and non-committal. He continued to hold out the handfuls of money.

Skid squirmed, looked at me, looked the airplane and then at Melville.

"Six thousand. If you can come up with $6,000 cash, she's yours." He didn't look happy.

Melville slowly put the two wads of money together in one hand and reached into his back pocket with the other. He pulled out another roll of money.

"Six thousand dollars," he said.

Skid took the money. "As is, where is," he declared. "You can put your own air in the tires." He turned to me and shook the money in my face. "And don't even think about a finder's fee. This guy's a thief, not a customer."

I wanted to speak. The dumb little farmer had demonstrated more salesmanship, control and respect in one stubby finger than Sicamore had in his whole body. I wanted to tell him that but it was Melville's moment. I said nothing.

"We have a deal, Mr. Sicamore," Melville said. He held out his hand.

Skid hesitated as if he wasn't going to lower himself to shake the grubby paw. He grabbed it and gave it a quick pump. "I'll get the paperwork from the car," he said.

85

"Do you have the keys, Skid?" I asked.

As he turned to go, he reached into his trench coat pocket, pulled them out and threw them at me. I caught them and handed them to Melville. He carefully unlocked the right front door, opened it and climbed in. He slid over to the left seat. I held the door open and looked inside. It was musty but the upholstery and instrument panel appeared to be in good shape. Melville gripped the control wheel in his left hand and peered through the dirt-streaked windshield.

"Well, Melville, what do you think?"

He didn't reply right away. I looked at him. There were tears welling up in his eyes. "It's mine," was all he said.

Chapter Fourteen

VING ON TOP

I watched through the office window while a Cessna One Seventy-two was taxied onto The Flying Circus ramp and shut down. The pilot jumped out and marched smartly toward the office. He was a lean, middle-aged man. I had seen the airplane before at the flying club but I didn't know the pilot. Henry was standing next to the door when he burst in.

"George Heinkle here," the pilot said, thrusting his hand at Henry. "Are you one of the owners?"

"Good morning. I'm Henry Rains," Henry said, accepting the handshake. "I'm one of the owners of The Flying Circus. This is my partner." Henry gestured in my direction.

Heinkle turned, crossed the room in three great strides, grabbed my hand and shook it with two crisp pumps. "George Heinkle," he said. He spoke with a slight German accent.

"Pleased to meet you," I replied.

"This is our office manager, Leanne Rains," Henry said, indicating Leanne behind the flight desk.

Heinkle stepped in that direction and gave Leanne the same snappy handshake. "A pleasure, Mrs. Rains," he said.

"Call me Leanne," she replied.

Heinkle clicked his heels and nodded in reply. He then turned toward Henry and me.

"I own the Cessna 172," he said. He spoke in quick, clipped sentences. "You need an airplane with the ving on top for sightseeing flights. I lease you mine. It vill carry four people. You do sightseeing, aerial photography, pipeline patrol and charter."

He didn't wait for a reply. "I lease it to you dry at $10 per hour, no minimum. Payments, you make every month vithin 30 days," Heinkle said. "I pay the first inspection by your mechanic, then you take care of everything except the engine overhaul and paint. Do ve have a deal?"

I thought the guy was too pushy for my taste. The school was

"You need an airplane with the ving on top."

getting busy enough for another airplane and the man was right
about the extra capabilities that a high-wing Cessna would give
our operation. Leanne had recently announced that the interest on
our hangar loan, which floated with the prime rate, had gone up a
full percentage point. That would make it tougher to borrow more
money to buy another airplane. Heinkle's offer was better than we
were paying to lease our older Cherokees but I was not the kind
of guy who could make a deal in thirty seconds.

"Would you like a coffee, Mr. Heinkle?" Henry asked.

"No thank you," he replied. "You call me George. I take you out
to see the airplane."

He turned on his heels, opened the door and gave a slight nod.
Henry and I looked at each other. "After you," I said and bowed my
head like Heinkle.

When we had cleared the door, the aircraft owner was already
half way to the airplane. The Cessna was not new but it was clean
inside and out. The paint had been touched up and the interior
upholstery had been replaced. It was an amateur job but the fabric
was new. The registration on the tail was C-LUFT. Heinkle was a

good salesman. He stood back and said nothing.

"Would you fly the airplane during the lease?" Henry asked.

"No. I'm in construction and too busy for the next six months. If you fly it a lot, I'll buy another vun in the fall. If not, I take it back."

It seemed like a good offer. Heinkle had covered all the bases. We either wanted to lease the airplane or not. Henry looked at me. I nodded.

"Very good, George," Henry said extending his hand. "We'll lease it for six months. I'll arrange the insurance, the inspection and I'll draft an agreement. I'll call you when we're ready for the airplane."

George shook his hand. "No need to call," he said. He reached into the airplane and pulled out the logbooks. "I'll sign the registration now and leave you the airplane. The handshake was our agreement. Send me the bill for the inspection."

He handed Henry a business card. He shook my hand, turned and marched across the ramp toward the flying club parking lot. The whole episode had taken less than five minutes and we had ourselves another airplane with the "ving on top".

Chapter Fifteen

SUMMER SALTS

We had a problem. The classified advertisements in the personal columns worked too well. The extra business kept Henry and me flying all the time and prevented us from teaching Barry McDay his instructor course. He kept busy by fueling and cleaning the airplanes and talking to customers but until he finished the training, he could only do checkouts, introductory flights and sightseeing rides.

A rainy day gave us a break. We couldn't fly but Barry and I used the time for him to practise ground briefings. Ray Tragunno walked into the office at the end of one. Ray was a workmate during my days at Derry Air. He now flew for Major Airlines as a second officer on a Boeing 747. He liked to hang around small airports when the weather was bad because there were always flying instructors available to buy him coffee and talk. Ray was one of the reasons that Henry and I had decided to go into the flying school business instead of the airlines. It had been an eye opener to see him stuck in the jumbo jet's engineer's seat without flying.

Barry and I joined Ray for a coffee.

"Ray, this is Barry McDay. He's working on his Instructor's Rating."

"The patter sounded familiar." Ray spoke in deep, slow tones. He had the ideal airline pilot voice. "Pleased to meet you."

"A pleasure," Barry said.

"Ray worked with Henry and me at Derry Air," I explained to Barry, "until Major Airlines hired him to do nothing in a 747 and get paid big money."

Ray ignored the barb. "Tell me," he said, "how's this little venture of yours going?" The tone of the question was not condescending but it was close.

"Ray, you wouldn't believe it," I said.

"No, I probably won't, but you're going to tell me anyway, aren't you?"

"We're so busy," I continued, "that we had to hire Henry's wife full time just to count the money." I was exaggerating but Ray liked a joke. I also knew his income was fixed and that it would bug him to think someone was making lots of money in private enterprise. "The trouble is," I continued, "we don't have time to spend it. The money keeps piling up in the bank while we're stuck flying every day."

Ray sipped his coffee before replying. "You're full of shit," he said. He was right.

"Ray, is your Instructor Rating still valid?" Barry asked.

"It might be. Why?"

"We're busy here. These guys are having trouble doing my course."

"It's true, Ray," I added. "We could use your instructing help, at least until Barry gets his rating."

"Not me," Ray replied. "I defied death enough to last a life-time."

"You're giving Barry the wrong impression," I said.

"He's young. He'll think it's exciting to be stuck in a cockpit with a series of ham-handed students intent on killing him."

"So you won't even consider a day or two a week?"

"Never in a million years."

I let the suggestion drop. We talked about his airline flying. A few minutes later a pretty girl about college age bounced through the office door. She was wearing a bright yellow rain slicker, sneakers and well-fitted jeans. The three of us stared while she closed the door and flipped off her hood, unleashing a bouncy pony tail. She unzipped the jacket. Underneath was a T-shirt advertising Monterrey Beach.

She looked at the three of us gawking and gave us a big smile.

"Good morning," she said in a cheerful husky voice.

Ray stood up. The tall, dark, handsome and married airline pilot walked toward her. "Good morning to you," he said in an extra friendly voice.

The girl tilted her head back to look at him as he approached. She held the smile. "Welcome to the Flying Circus," he said, extending his hand. She accepted the handshake. "I'm Ray Tragunno. I'm one of the flying instructors here." He made it sound important.

The girl looked quickly at Barry and me and then back to Ray.

91

"Welcome to The Flying Circus."

"Sarenna Salts," she replied. "My friends call me Summer."

I watched Monterrey Beach on the T-shirt rise and set with each breath that the young girl took. I missed the joke in the name. So did Ray.

"Well, I'd like to be your friend, Summer," Ray said smoothly. "Are you interested in flying?"

"I'm interested in everything," she replied.

"Cool. Let me show you an outline of the pleasure pilot's course."

Without taking his eyes off her, Ray held his hand out behind him. It was obviously my cue to produce the outline.

"Do you live around here?" Ray asked.

"I go to the university," she replied.

"That's interesting," he said. "What course are you taking?"

"Sports medicine," she said and then added, "with a major in gymnastics."

I started to catch on. She called herself Summer Salts and was majoring in gymnastics; this girl was either living a humorous coincidence or she was killing us with one-liners. I gave Ray a course handout.

"Have a seat and I'll go over this with you," Ray said, gesturing to one of the classroom tables. "Would you like a coffee?"

"No thank you."

As she sat down, she smiled at Barry and me. I smiled back. Barry gave her a nod. Ray pretended that we didn't exist. He read the course outline to her. Then he explained that he'd like to take her up on an introductory flight but the weather was not suitable. "I help out here one or two days a week," he said. "The rest of the time I fly a Boeing 747 for Major Airlines out of Toronto."

"That's fascinating," Summer said. She made it sound genuine. "It's wonderful that you take the time to teach others how to fly."

"It's the least I can do," Ray replied. "Let's see if we can schedule a flying lesson for you when I'm available again."

Leanne and Henry were taking a day off so there was no one else to help Ray with the booking sheets. He introduced Barry and me. When Barry shook Summer's hand, he said, "I'm sure Captain Tragunno will take good care of you."

"I hope so," she replied with a big smile.

Ray drew her attention to the schedule. "Tomorrow I'll be flying a 747 to England but I'll be back on Friday. Would you be available then?"

"Friday afternoon would be fine," she said.

I booked them an airplane. Summer endured a few more minutes of small talk from Ray and then said goodbye.

When she was leaving, Ray watched her go all the way to the parking lot. I was the first to speak.

"Well, Mr. Cool, you handled that very well."

"Just trying to help out," he replied.

"So, how many days a week can you give us?"

"Well, let's wait and see if Summer is going to take flying lessons."

"No deal. You either sign up for at least two full days a week of instructing or I'll let the younger, more single Barry McDay fly with little Miss Monterrey Beach on Friday."

"You're blackmailing me."

"Not quite," I replied. "Blackmail is when I threaten to call Helga and tell her you're flying with cute young blondes in tight T-shirts."

"Okay and I'll pay for lesson number two."

Barry jumped into the conversation. "Try it for a few weeks, Ray. If you don't like it, I'll be ready to take over your customers. We get a lot of students from the university here."

The last comment swung it.

"Well, okay, for a couple of weeks, just to help out. Don't get the idea that I'm doing it just for the pretty girls."

"Never in a million years, Ray," I said. "Never in a million years."

After Ray left, Barry said, "Little Miss Monterrey Beach isn't going to take flying lessons."

"What makes you so sure?"

"Her name's Summer but it's not Salts, it's McDay," he said with a grin. "She's my sister."

"Why didn't you say so when she was here?" I exclaimed.

"I was having too much fun watching her handle Mr. Macho Airline Pilot," he said. "I didn't want to spoil it."

94

"Well, her timely visit landed us another flying instructor. You say she doesn't want to take flying lessons?"

"No. She was here just for a friendly visit. Flying is not exciting enough for her. She is more of the skydiving type. I told her to drop by and say 'Hello' anytime it was raining and she was bored with school."

"Do you want to cancel her introductory lesson?"

"No, in fact I'll pay for it," he said. "We want to keep Ray interested."

"Okay and I'll pay for lesson number two."

"You're on. I'll talk to her."

Chapter Sixteen

NIGHT FRIGHT

Melville and I flew to Derry Air with Barry in one of our Cherokee 140s to take delivery of Melville's TriPacer. The young farmer was excited. "I named 'er 'Petunia'," Melville told us as he sawed away at the controls during the flight, "after my mom. I think I've talked my dad into building a strip on the farm," he said. He turned toward us each time he spoke.

"That must have taken a lot of persuading, Melville," I replied. "Now look ahead and try to fly a heading."

"Not really," he said. "Dad's thinking about lessons."

It was a scary thought. It had been fun teaching Melville even though he had taken over 100 hours to finish his pilot licence. I had met his dad. He would take longer. Ebert Passmore was an unteachable farmer who knew it all. I knew because he had told me.

"We'll have to introduce your dad to Barry," I said. "He'll have his Instructor's Rating soon."

Melville turned around. "You'd like teaching my dad," he said to Barry. The airplane zoomed skyward. "He knows lots about flying already."

I looked at Barry sitting across the two jump seats in the back. He was turning green from the airplane's gyrations.

"I'll look forward to meeting him," Barry lied through clenched teeth.

When we landed at Derry Airport, Melville and I hopped out. Barry climbed into the left seat and headed back to Circus.

We met Darcy, Derry Air's chief mechanic, in his office. He handed Melville the keys. He had been true to his word and had completed the annual inspection on the TriPacer for under $500. Melville paid him cash from the roll of money in his coveralls.

"Fly carefully and call me if you have any problems," Darcy said. It was the only time I had heard him speak to a pilot without being sarcastic. He obviously had a soft spot for the round little farmer.

Melville barely heard him. He gave a quick "Thank you," and ran out the door to the airplane.

"Darcy, I can't believe it," I said with a smile. "You were being nice."

He waved the handful of bills in my face. "Hey," he said with a crooked grin, "we don't give respect around here, it's earned."

I followed Melville's path out the door. The TriPacer was parked in the middle of the ramp. Darcy's shop had scrubbed the grim off. The yellow and red stripes gleamed in the sunshine. The little airplane looked like a clown in church next to the vanilla-colored Cessnas and Pipers. Melville sat grinning in the pilot seat. I let him enjoy it while I took a close look at the outside. The TriPacer was a lot more appealing without the flat tires and dirt streaks. The recover job was in good shape. The stitches in the fabric were straight and neatly taped and doped over. I opened the cowlings. The engine compartment had been sprayed clean and shiny.

Melville climbed out. "How's she look?" His beaming face dictated a positive response.

"Melville, you robbed that poor aircraft broker blind. You should be proud."

He was.

We did the walkaround together and climbed in. I thought that switching to the TriPacer would be a handful for Melville. The older high-wing airplane was different from the Cherokee 140. I was wrong. It was the perfect farmer's airplane. It was strong as a milk stool and handled like a tractor. While taxiing out to the runway it was obvious that the heavy nosewheel steering suited Melville. On the way back to Circus I had him practise steep turns, slow flight and stalls. The fat stubby wings rewarded his coarse inputs with a suitable lack of response. By the time we had completed some circuits at the Circus Airport, Melville had overcome his excitement and was flying the airplane well. I sent him solo. He was gone a long time, no doubt buzzing his parents' farm. About the time I started to worry, he came back. He climbed out of the TriPacer grinning from ear to ear.

Later that week, we continued Melville's Night Rating Course on his airplane. The short wings caused the TriPacer to descend rapidly when the power was reduced. It was a hard airplane to land smoothly in daylight. On the approach the pilot had one brief opportunity to pull back at precisely the right moment to arrest the descent before hitting the runway. At night, the approach was like riding a crowbar down a well. The almost total lack of shock absorbing in the landing gear sent a jarring signal to the inaccurate pilot's backside.

Melville caught on quickly. After two night landings, he was greasing the TriPacer onto the runway between the two rows of lights stretching into the darkness. He was soon ready for the last dual lesson on the Night Rating Course, the crosscountry flight. For this, we flew around the western end of Lake Ontario, through the Toronto International Terminal Control Area to the Toronto Island Airport. The lesson provided some night navigation practice as well as radio work in a high-density traffic environment.

"When we go to Toronto," Melville asked excitedly, "will I be talking to the same controllers who speak to the airline pilots?"

"Yes you will."

"Do I call them, 'sir'?"

"No, definitely not, you talk to them just like you're an airline pilot."

"Wow!"

I was worried about the radio work for this trip because of Melville's long wind-up before talking. The dead airtime was okay at Circus where the controllers recognized Melville's voice. They'd wait through his pauses. The rapid-fire Toronto controllers were too busy for such special treatment.

I scripted the anticipated radio conversation for the Toronto Terminal Control Area and into the Toronto Island Airport. I wrote down everything that I thought Melville would have to say and what he should hear in response. We practised on the ground before the trip. Melville read his part and I played the air traffic controller.

On the evening of our flight we reviewed the script and filed a round-robin flight plan to Toronto Island. Melville checked his equipment: two flashlights, two pencils, a map and the script. We did the pre-flight inspection together and climbed in. Melville went through the checklist, started the engine and picked up the microphone for taxi instructions. He keyed the mic, took a deep breath, looked both ways, licked his lips, pulled in his tongue and spoke from his boots, "Circus ground, this is Lima Oscar Whiskey November?"

"Hi, Melville. I see you're on a flight plan to Toronto. Taxi for Runway 24, wind calm, altimeter 30.03. Call me on the tower frequency when you're ready to takeoff."

It was Barry in the tower. So much for proper radio procedure training.

"Okay, Barry, thanks," Melville replied. Then he looked at me. "I mean, Oscar Whiskey November, roger."

We took off from Runway 24 and headed for Derry on the way to Toronto. Barry bid us a "good flight" when Melville called clear of the Circus Control Zone. It was a calm, clear night. We cruised along the Lake Ontario shoreline. Navigation was simply a case of identifying the next grouping of lights. Melville followed our progress with his tongue hanging out and a stubby finger on the map.

When we approached Derry where Melville had learned to fly, he called for permission to fly through the airport control zone.

"Derry tower, this is Lima Oscar Whiskey November?"

"Hi Melville, it's good to hear from you. How's the new airplane?"

The controller was Diana Bates. She had taken flying lessons when I worked at Derry Air.

Melville looked at me to see what he should say.

"Tell her that the new airplane is fine."

"The new airplane is fine, Diana," Melville said. The non-standard radio talk was making him grin. "I like it," he added and then looked at me. I nodded, he released the button.

"That's great. You're cleared through the zone along the lakeshore. The altimeter is 30.04. Call me when you're leaving the area."

"Okay, I mean, roger, Oscar Whiskey November."

The end of Lake Ontario was outlined by the lights of Derry. We turned right and headed for Toronto. After we had called clear of the Derry Control Zone, Melville tuned in the frequency for the Toronto tape-recorded terminal information service. He copied down the numbers on his kneeboard. Then he changed the frequency to Toronto Terminal Control. It was busy.

"Air Canada 1018 now cleared to twelve thousand, break, break, Air Mexico turn right to zero six zero."

The controller was working both IFR and VFR air traffic around Toronto. We couldn't hear the airline replies. They were speaking to him on a different frequency.

"Canadian 800 over to the tower now, one eighteen four."

"Hotel Delta Alpha, one more turn for the localizer, keep your speed up, sir, there's a 747 behind you."

The radio work was rapid and continuous. I looked at Melville. His eyes were wide.

"You just have to jump in when he's not talking, Melville." I said. "He can listen to two conversations at once. You just have to say exactly what we practised. Start by making initial contact."

He stared at his kneeboard, keyed the microphone, took a deep breath, licked his lips, pulled in his tongue, looked both ways and spoke, "Toronto Terminal, this is Lima Oscar Whiskey November?" He said it as a question. He looked at me, I nodded and he released the mic button.

"American 2320, radar contact, now cleared to 12,000."

Melville gave me a blank stare. The tongue was at full hang.

"Just wait, if he heard you, he'll call back."

"Tango Charlie Gulf over to Island Tower now, one eighteen two."

"Tango Charlie Gulf."

"Is that Oscar Whiskey November on one nineteen four?"

Melville looked at me and did nothing.

"Say 'Affirmative'," I said.

Mic on, breath in, lick lips, tongue in, look and, "Affirmative."

"Air Canada 1018, cleared to Flight Level two five zero, contact Cleveland Centre."

Melville gave me the startled deer look again.

"He'll call you, just wait," I said.

"Hotel Delta Alpha, right turn to 200 degrees to intercept the localizer for 24 Right, you're cleared for the approach."

"That must be Melville in Oscar Whiskey November," the controller said. "Good evening. Squawk ident."

Melville was paralyzed. I pushed the identification button on the transponder.

"Air Canada 1214 heavy, radar contact. You're number two to 24 Right behind a Merlin intercepting the localizer.

"Radar contact Oscar Whiskey November. Circus said you're going to the Island. It looks like a nice night for it. Stay along the lakeshore, not above 2,000 and call me when you reach Humber Bay. Do you know where that is?"

Melville looked down at the now unnecessary script on his knee-board and then at me.

"Say 'Affirmative'."

"Affirmative."

That was it. Barry must have called the Terminal controller from Circus and filled him in about the slow farmer in the TriPacer. The call by Humber Bay would be to switch over to the Toronto Island Control Tower. There was nothing else to do but fly along, listen to the steady stream of radio chatter and enjoy the solid carpet of lights below that was Metropolitan Toronto.

Melville continued to hold the microphone in front of his face ready to transmit again.

"We're out of gas!" Melville exclaimed.

"That's it for now, Melville," I said. "Fly the airplane and don't get lost."

Melville followed our progress along the map. When we were approaching Humber Bay, the Terminal controller called us.

"Oscar Whiskey November, I see you're coming up to the Humber. Call Island Tower now, one one eight decimal two. I'll talk to you on your way back."

I pointed to the reply on the radio script. Melville keyed the microphone. "Oscar Whiskey November."

As soon as he spoke, the lights in the cockpit went out. We stared at each other in the dark.

"Where's your flashlight, Melville?"

He dug in the map pocket on his side of the airplane. I took the microphone from him. I punched the transmit button and released. There was no click sound on the radio. We couldn't hear the controller's voice talking to us or to anyone else. The engine continued to buzz along. We had lost our electrical system.

Melville turned on his flashlight.

"Shine it on the engine instruments," I said.

He did. The alternator output gauge read zero. So did the fuel quantity gauges in the same instrument cluster.

"We're out of gas!" Melville exclaimed. There was more doubt than panic in his voice.

His reaction was typical of a new pilot. He was responding without thinking. The fuel gauges were electric. Having no electrics over downtown Toronto at night was a serious situation but it was not yet life threatening. I was determined to make it a learning experience for Melville.

"What should we do?" I asked.

"Declare an emergency?"

"Did you fill up the tanks before we took off?"

"Yes."

"Did you check them on the walkaround inspection?"

"Yes."

"Is the engine running?"

"Yes."

"Are we out of gas?"

He scratched his head. "No."

"What drives the fuel gauges?"

He shone the light on them. "Electricity?"

"What drives the lights?"

"Electricity."

102

He shone the light on the alternator gauge. "The alternator isn't working," he said.

"What should we do?" I asked.

He recited the air regulations. "Inform ATC and land as soon as possible."

"Does our radio work?"

Melville turned the squelch knob up on the radio volume to listen for background static. There was none.

"No."

"What should we do?"

"Squawk 7600 on the transponder and land at the nearest airport."

"Go ahead. I'll fly the airplane."

I took over control of the TriPacer. While talking, we had been flying along the lakeshore toward Toronto's downtown Island Airport. It was now less than five miles ahead. I set up a descent.

Melville shone his light on the radar transponder and gingerly tuned it to 7600, the radio failure code.

"Does it work?" I asked.

He turned the transponder selector to test. The light didn't come on.

"No."

He scratched his head again. "If the alternator is off, all the electrics are dead."

"Now you're getting warm," I said. "What about the battery?"

"It should carry some electrics for awhile."

"But it didn't. What should we do?"

While Melville thought, I flew over the middle of the Island Airport. The lights of the high rise office towers loomed on our left and the cold, black nothingness of Lake Ontario stretched out to our right. The biggest danger was our lack of running lights. No lights inside meant no lights outside. The unlit, fabric-covered TriPacer was invisible, even to radar operators. My objective was to land at the Island Airport without getting run over by another airplane.

"We should land as soon as possible?" Melville asked.

"Probably, but on the way down, try the auxiliary master electric switch."

Melville reached under his seat to the switch on the front of the battery box. As soon as he touched it, he yanked his fingers back.

"It's hot!" he yelped.

103

"Then turn it off. Use the end of your flashlight."

He knocked the switch to the neutral position.

I looked out the windshield. I could see the navigation lights of two airplanes on the left downwind leg of the circuit for Runway 26. I turned to follow them. If everything went according to government decree, the Island Airport controllers would be expecting us to show up even though we were out of radio contact. The two airplanes ahead would be warned about us and cleared to land. All other traffic in the area would be told to remain clear until we either arrived, showed up somewhere else or had run out of gas according to the fuel time on our flight plan.

"What now?" Melville asked. His voice was calm but worried.

"We'll follow those two airplanes in for a landing," I said, pointing out the traffic. "You have control."

"I have control," he replied.

The airplanes ahead did full stop landings. A green light was pointed at us from the control tower when we were on the base leg. The controllers must have spotted us against the night sky. Melville turned over Toronto harbor and lined up with the lights for Runway 26. He did a good landing without a landing light, something we had practised the week before at Circus. A flashing green light from the tower cleared us to taxi in. We shut down in front of the fixed base operator.

I had no idea what had caused the electric failure but it felt good to have things work out. We were stuck in Toronto but the little farmer probably learned a lot. So did I. The government decreed system worked.

I figured Melville needed a little time to relax. "I'll go in and call the control tower on the telephone," I said to him as we climbed out, "and then we'll see if we can locate the problem."

I walked across the ramp to the fuel dealer office which was also a flying school. Inside, there were several people standing around. They stared at me when I walked through the door. A lineman standing behind the flight desk was the first to speak. "The tower wants you to call," he said pointing to a telephone on the counter. "You can use the direct line."

"Thank you."

I picked up the phone.

"Tower here," a voice said on the other end.

"Hi. It's the pilot from Oscar Whiskey November," I said a little

104

nervously. "Thanks for the visual landing clearance."

"You're welcome," he said. He sounded friendly enough. "I gather you had an electrical problem."

"Yes sir. I don't know what happened but we'll check it out."

"Okay," he said. "I'll hang on to the return portion of your flight plan until you let me know what you're going to do."

"Fine, thank you," I replied.

I didn't have a plan. It was after ten o'clock. There would be no maintenance open in Toronto. Calling Darcy at home and telling him to drive to Toronto was high on my wish list but I could guess his reply. Melville was going to learn that operating your own airplane could include the cost of an unscheduled stay at an expensive downtown hotel followed by a morning meeting with a big-dollar Toronto aircraft mechanic.

I went back outside. Melville had the engine top cowlings open and the front seat cushion out on the ground. He was standing by the front of the airplane with a screwdriver in his hand and his tongue hanging out.

"Melville, what are you doing?"

He sucked in his tongue. "I think I found the problem. The batt'ry was hot," he said, pointing to the front seat with the screwdriver, "so I looked at the starter." He stepped back and rotated the propeller a quarter turn. I could hear that the starter was still engaged. "The starter gear stayed in when we were flyin'," Melville said. He stuck his tongue out and looked at me to see if he should continue.

"Why would a stuck starter gear blow the whole electric system?" I asked.

"When the engin' turns the starter, it makes it a generator," he explained. "The extra electricity goes to the batt'ry."

At this point he hustled around to the right front door of the airplane. He leaned in and looked back at me. "The starter solenoid should protect the batt'ry from too much electricity but it got too hot and stuck." He tapped the offending solenoid on the front of the battery box for emphasis. "The batt'ry overheated."

I realized that now I was the student and Melville was the teacher. "So we'll get it fixed in the morning," I said.

Melville bustled around the wing strut to the front of the airplane. He waved the screwdriver at the nose. "If we push back the starter gear with the screwdriver, we can hand-prop the airplane. The alternator'll give us electric power," Melville explained, "if the batt'ry is not all dead. We don't know for sure 'til we run the engin'."

He was making sense.

"So we run the engine by hand starting it to see if the alternator will supply electricity. If the battery hasn't been killed completely, it should."

"I think so," he said.

"If the battery isn't dead, it should power the electrics with the engine shut off, right?"

"Yah, but we don't wanna kill the batt'ry by trying it."

"Okay, I think you're right but I'm going to call Darcy for a second opinion."

"Sure."

I thought a family man who started work at eight o'clock in the morning might be in bed at 10:30. He wasn't. He answered the phone on the first ring.

"Well sky pilot, what are you wrecking now?"

I explained what had happened and what we planned to do. I could hear one of Darcy's pre-school kids making baby talk on his knee. "Is that you or the baby making the comments?" I asked.

"Junior and I are watching 'Halloween'. It's his favorite movie. Melville's right. Those starters have a history of doing that. I should have changed the Bendix when we had it in the shop. If the battery is not completely melted, you should be all right to fly home."

"I was hoping for a little more than a 'should be'," I replied.

"Try the battery with just the cockpit lights on. If it will hold those, then hand-start the engine. If the alternator comes on line, go for it. The worst that can happen is losing electric power again."

"I appreciate your confidence."

"It's only because you've got Melville to help you." I could hear him smile.

"Okay, we'll try it."

"Call me after you land at Circus."

"It'll be midnight."

"We'll be up. The movie just started."

I went back outside and related the conversation to Melville. We turned on the battery and cockpit lights. They worked. Melville went to the front of the airplane with the screwdriver and turned the Bendix drive back into the starter. We reinstalled the engine cowling and the front seat and did a walkaround inspection. With

106

Melville in the pilot seat, I hand started the engine by swinging the propeller. I climbed into the right seat. Melville pointed to the alternator gauge. It was working.

"Okay," I said, "load it up with the lights and radios we need and see if it holds."

It did.

Melville used the script to call Toronto Island Ground Control for taxi instructions for the flight back to Circus. There was no other traffic.

"I see you got her working," the controller said and then gave us a clearance to the runway.

Melville did the pre-takeoff checks. The alternator was holding. The master switch stayed cool. We launched into the night.

Toronto Terminal Control was not as busy. Melville had little trouble fitting in his transmissions. When we had cleared that area twenty minutes later, the radio work was done. Derry and Circus Towers closed for the night by 11:00 p.m. The weather was clear and calm. The rest of the flight was smooth sailing along the lakeshore.

We landed at Circus and put the airplane away. I called Darcy.

"City morgue, you stab them, we slab them," he said.

"Hi Jason, we're in Circus."

"Tell Melville that I'll be down in the morning with a new starter, solenoid and battery. I'll install them no charge."

"That's very generous of you."

"No, it's called sucking up to a good customer after screwing up. Besides, it's worth it after thinking of you working on the ramp and getting your fingers dirty," he chuckled.

"Well I appreciated your going out on a limb and giving us a maintenance release over the phone."

"Who's calling?" he laughed.

Chapter Seventeen

SUNDAY FARMER

I didn't get home from work until late most nights. It made for an abbreviated family life. Susan never complained but her evenings alone had to hurt. We lived in a clapboard farmhouse an hour from The Flying Circus. We had bought the old place with the idea of fixing it up but our renovation plans went on permanent hold as soon as Henry and I launched the flying school. When window-panes fell out of their rotting frames I stuck them back in with duct tape. When the horses kicked out boards in their stalls I tied them up with binder twine. Our cars ran rough and the acre of grass around the house grew long.

Life was not without its fun. I took Sundays off whether the flying school needed me or not. For part of the day, Susan and I ignored the uncut grass and made time for horseback riding with our neighbor, Gary Morningside. On any given Sunday afternoon a group of six to ten riders gathered at Gary's place for a trek into the bush not far away.

Gary was an aluminum siding salesman during the day and a cowboy at night. He fit both parts. He had a scrawny cowboy body, greased hair, toothpick-in-the-mouth smile, string tie, alligator boots and a ready sarcastic remark.

Gary kept quarter horses. He liked to ride and he loved to compete in local rodeos but his biggest passion was buying, selling or trading horses.

My horse was half thoroughbred and half Percheron. He was twice the size of any of Gary's mounts.

"You should wear a parachute ridin' that monster," he said looking up at me on one of our Sunday trail rides.

"This is a whole horse, Gary, not a quarter horse."

"This is a real horse," he countered. "One that'll race barrels under 20 seconds. That elephant of yers needs a whole county to turn around."

"Can your horse jump?" I asked.

"Jumpin' is for queers," he replied. "Let me get you a horse that can move, a quarter horse."

"Sunny is just fine," I said, patting my mount on the neck.

"I'll trade you even for my paint," Gary said.

"Ah ha. So you have a secret desire to own a full-sized horse."

"I have a secret desire to sell 'im for meat. There's a lot of cash ridin' on those elephant hooves."

Sunny ended the conversation by moving over on Gary's horse. He had to speed up to keep from being squeezed into the bush.

"Control that thing, will you!" Gary barked.

"He heard you, Gary. Now you're in big trouble. Elephants never forget."

"Two thousand dollars," he said without blinking an eye.

It was at Gary's farm that I found a solution to my long lawn. There was an old tractor parked behind his barn with a two-metre wide mower deck slung underneath. He obviously never used it since his grass-gone-wild looked like mine.

"Gary, what's with the tractor and mower?" I asked one day. We were leaning against his corral fence watching Susan give a lesson to one of his boarders.

109

"She's seized," he replied.

"Seized, as in 'rusted tight for forty years'?"

"I cut the grass when I first got 'er two years ago. Worked great but then I parked 'er for the winter. She hasn't run since."

I had no delusions about rebuilding the tractor. I didn't have the time, the money or the know-how but I had Melville.

"Want to sell it?"

During our conversation, Gary had been watching Susan and the girl she was teaching until he heard the word "sell". He turned and looked at me. "Maybe."

"How much do you want for it?"

He looked over at the tractor and then back at me. "Two thousand dollars," he said without blinking an eye.

I had been thinking of $150. It was my turn to make a counter offer but we were friends. I didn't want to insult him with a low-ball figure. "It's out of my league," I said.

There was nothing that Gary loved more than deal making. "The engine was all rebuilt when I bought 'er," he said, trying to keep the negotiations alive. "She's worth $4,000 runnin'."

"You may be right, Gary, but I don't have that kind of money to take a chance on a seized tractor. You keep it and my yard can continue to look like yours."

He was obviously disappointed that I wouldn't dicker.

The next day, Melville was at the airport giving his airplane its weekly wash. I asked him about the tractor.

"Melville, what do you know about an Avery Model A?"

Melville cocked his hip as if to lean on something that wasn't there, hung out his tongue, rubbed his forehead and looked at the ground. He transformed from an enthusiastic farm boy to sage old man before my eyes.

"Hercules engine?" he asked slowly, hauling in the tongue briefly.

"That's it."

"Never had one," he said. The tone of his voice indicated that he never would. "They're kinda small."

"My neighbor has one for sale with a Woods mower on it," I said. "I was thinking of it for cutting my grass."

His face brightened a little but he didn't respond right away. I waited.

"Should be all right for yard work," he finally announced. "They stopped making 'em a long time ago but the engine is common. Any other parts you need, you make."

"The engine was rebuilt two years ago," I said, "but it's seized from being parked outside all winter."

"Coal oil in the spark plug holes for a week and she'll run," he declared. This pronouncement was made like a doctor prescribing medicine for a bad cough. Then he added the standard farmer question. "How much does he want for it?"

"What do you think it's worth?"

He traced something in the gravel with the toe of his boot while holding an elbow with one hand and his jaw with the other. "Runnin', with a good mower, maybe $1,000," he said slowly. Then he squinted his eyes nearly shut. "I wouldn't offer him more than $500, as is."

"Okay, Melville, thank you."

He was obviously disappointed that I was ending the discussion so soon. He was just warming up. "I'll help you git it runnin'," he offered.

It was what I was hoping he would say. "Well, thank you, Melville. That's kind of you. I'll take you up on it if I can get the guy down from his price to yours."

"Tell him that tractors like that are parked behind barns everywhere. He should be happy to have you haul it away for nottin'."

"Thanks Melville."

The next Sunday Gary came over while Susan was giving a lesson in our corral. After the initial "Hellos", we leaned in silence. Gary was the next to speak.

"That little appaloosa of Susan's would make a good child's pony," he said.

Gary was referring to Glider. He was a young horse that Susan had purchased the year before. He had been underfed as a colt and had never properly developed. Susan had paid $50 to save him from the slaughterhouse. She used Glider for first-time riders because he never went faster than a walk no matter how hard he was prodded.

111

He spent most of his time as the barnyard pet. As Susan gained popularity as an instructor, she talked about replacing him with a horse that could do more but she didn't want to see him go for meat.

"Susan doesn't use 'im much," he said.

"You're right," I replied. I tried to sound noncommittal.

"Anytime you want one less hay burner in yer barn, I'll take 'im off yer hands."

"Good idea, Gary. He's yours."

He didn't expect that answer. He pushed his beat-up cowboy hat back on his head so he could see me better and then looked around to buy some time.

"How much?" he asked.

"Two thousand bucks," I answered without hesitation.

"Oh forget that!" he exclaimed. He pushed back from the fence rail, whipped his hat off and slapped his leg with it. "That horse can barely walk."

"You're right, Gary," I said with a smile. "He'd be worth $4,000 running."

He was about to jump up and down to show his disbelief but he stopped himself. A grin grew across his leathery face. "You thinkin' of tradin' a seized tractor for a seized horse?"

"Sounds good to me."

He calmly stuck out his hand, "You gotta deal."

I shook his hand. "Agreed."

We both went back to leaning on the fence, grinning to ourselves. After awhile, I broke the happy silence, "Who's going to tell Susan?"

"Oh not me," he said, shaking his head vigorously. "She's your woman; you gotta tell 'er."

"Okay, but if she says 'No', the deal's off."

Susan had succeeded in the fashion business by being perceptive. Lazy or dishonest employees could run but they could not hide. Susan spotted them right away. She could see through me just as well. I waited until after work the next evening before saying anything about the deal.

Susan was already home when I got there. She seemed to be in an extra good mood. Dinner was ready and it was not the usual macaroni and cheese. She had picked up steaks and wine on the way home. She hummed and smiled while serving them up. It seemed like a good time to talk tractors.

"Honey," I said smoothly, "Gary said he was interested in Glider."

"I figured you two were up to something."

"What do you mean?" I tried to sound innocent.

"You and Gary talked during my whole lesson yesterday and now you just called me 'Honey' for the third time in three years."

"He's willing to trade his tractor/mower for Glider."

"You mean the seized old rig behind his barn?"

"Yes, but don't get me wrong. I'm just thinking about it. Of course, the deal would have to be okay with you."

"Which one of you cooked up this up?"

"We both did. Gary wants the horse and I want the tractor."

"And the tractor doesn't work."

"Right. Either does the horse. Melville Passmore said he would help me get the tractor running."

"Well then go for it," she replied calmly as we sat down to eat, so calmly that I missed it at first.

"It has a huge mower," I continued, "I'll be able to cut the grass in 20 min. . . . what did you say?"

"I said 'go for it.'" She was grinning from ear to ear.

"Just like that? Glider is your horse. If you'd rather not, it's okay with me."

"A farm like ours needs a tractor," she said still smiling. "We can use it to fix fences, pull a wagon and yank out stumps, right?"

"Yah, that's just what I was going to say."

"And Gary will strap a cute saddle on Glider and sell him for big money to some horse-dumb parents of a spoiled rich kid who are looking for a quiet pony, right?"

"Probably. How did you know?"

"I've known Gary as long as you have. Make the deal as long as Glider doesn't go for meat."

Susan was being too good to be true. There was something that I was missing but I couldn't tell from across the dinner table.

"Wouldn't you rather trade Glider for a better horse?"

"I thought about that and decided it would be better to have one less in the barn for now."

The grin was still there. The tone in her voice indicated that she was playing with me.

"What am I missing?"

"Ask me how my day went."

"How was your day, Honey?"

"Fine," she said coyly.

113

"Was it extra fine?" I asked.

"Yes."

"Are you going to tell me?"

"Hymie came into the store today and offered me a district manager's job."

"You're kidding! What district manager's job?"

"All of Ontario." Her face was all smiles.

"Wow, that's fantastic! What brought that on?"

"My good work, of course," she said. She was trying to act indignant while beaming at the same time. The beaming won.

"He told me that he liked the changes I had made to my store. He noted that my sales figures were way up and asked me if I thought I could work the same magic on all the stores in Ontario."

"This is really exciting news. I feel stupid for mentioning the tractor. When does all this happen?"

"Well, first of all, I didn't say I'd take the job," she said seriously. I gave her a puzzled look. "Well, it represents quite a change for us. I'll be travelling a lot, including some overnight stays in towns further away."

"What did you tell the man?"

"I said that I'd have to think about it."

"Ooh. You are a gutsy lady."

She blushed. "Well, I did want to talk to you about it. Besides, in the fashion business, it's not cool to be a 'yes man'."

Susan had never been anyone's "yes man".

"Now I know why you're doing so well."

She blushed more. "We should discuss it. With this job I won't be at home as much. I'll have to cut back on the riding lessons. This is a complete change in direction."

"And on the other hand?"

"It represents more financial security for us. My salary goes up 30 per cent and I get a company car."

"And you run the largest district of one of the biggest ladies wear chains. Doesn't that scare you?"

"No!"

"That's my girl. So you have to decide to be a riding instructor or retailing tycoon. If you're asking me, I'd say the opportunity to teach riding will always be there. I'm not home as much either so don't worry about me."

"That's what I thought," she said pensively.

114

"When do you have to let him know?"

"In the morning."

"What are you going to say?"

Her face split into a wide grin. She came over, sat on my knee, gave me a big hug and said, "I'm going to say that my husband is trading away my horses for broken farm equipment so I might as well take the job."

I tickled her. She screamed and jumped up. I raised my wineglass, "Here's to steak every night," I said.

She raised hers, "Here's to your cooking it."

Chapter Eighteen

WHALE REVIVED

Darcy Philips finished Dave's Lake amphibian and delivered it to The Flying Circus. The airplane looked great. It had new paint, windows, interior, instruments and radios. The electrics, hydraulics and engine had been overhauled. According to Dave's instructions to the paint shop, the vertical fin sported a caricature of a tooth with wings. The caption, "The Tooth Ferry" was painted on the rudder. The bill for all the work had come to $39,000.

I spoke to Darcy before he flew back to Derry with one of our Cherokees for an inspection.

"How's it fly now?" I asked enthusiastically.

"Like a whale," he replied.

"Come on, Darcy," I said with a nervous laugh, "Michelin is paying you all that money to fix his airplane and all you can say is that it flies 'like a whale'?"

Darcy drew an impatient breath and said, "If you took an ugly boat, added wings, pontoons and wheels, placed the Statue of Liberty on top and powered it with a 180-horsepower engine pointed backwards, how do you think it would fly?"

"I don't know."

"Like a whale."

He was serious.

"Why did you fix it if it wasn't going to fly any better?"

"Because you told me to. Everything works and the airplane looks good but it still flies like a whale."

Darcy departed, leaving me to face Dave on my own. We were scheduled to fly that afternoon. He was in the lounge when I returned from a lesson with another student. He was holding court on our couch armed with a box of jelly donuts and his bag of weak jokes. Whiskey lay on the floor ringed with confectionery fallout.

"Why do they name an army knife after a country that hasn't been to war in 500 years?"

116

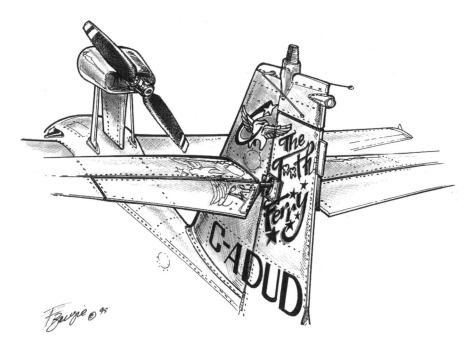

The vertical fin sported a caricature of a tooth with wings.

"I don't know," Leanne replied.

"Beats me too," Dave said, biting into a rhubarb-cream delight. The donut left a powered sugar ring around his mouth.

"Hey," he said to me between chews, "the airplane looks great! I can't wait to fly it!"

"Just remember Dave, a lot of the overhaul money was spent on things like paint and radios. They won't make the airplane perform any better."

Dave wasn't listening. "I bet she really goes!"

He was going to find out the hard way. "Well, let's try it and see," I said.

"I'll just go to the washroom first," he said, heaving himself off the couch. "You check it over and we'll be right out."

Whiskey started eating the donuts on the floor around him without getting up. I signed the log sheet and went outside.

"Pull back!" I bellowed into the headset as we barreled down the runway on the takeoff.

"I am!" Dave yelled back.

There was no panic in his shout but there was in mine. The Lake was approaching the halfway mark on the 5,000-foot runway. We were well beyond the airplane's published rotation point.

"Pull harder!" I barked.

The rpm and manifold pressure gauges indicated we were pulling maximum power but the flying boat was accelerating worse than a cruise ship. At 3,000 feet of runway I was about to call an abort when the nosewheel started to rise.

"Don't let it come up too high!" I yelled.

Dave relaxed some of his back pressure. We rolled along the runway with the nose up for another 1,000 feet. The airspeed indicator advanced like the minute hand on a clock but the main wheels finally lifted off. We were flying.

The Lake hung in ground effect as it accelerated slowly. The end of the runway flashed by. I reached over and selected the landing gear lever "up". I could visualize the wheels slowly retracting into the wings and the hull. The "gear up" light came on just as we scraped over the fence.

The takeoff seemed all too familiar. I couldn't see any performance gains from Dave's $39,000 renovations. I looked over at him. Dave was hunched over the control wheel and grinning from ear to ear.

"She's a lot better!" he whooped. "We're really flying!"

It was a $39,000 thing to say.

"Barely," I thought to myself.

"I'll turn a bit to miss the trees," he offered.

"Good idea," I yelled in reply.

Whiskey watched ahead as we skimmed over the corn. He was sitting on the rear seats with his front legs on the floor and his head resting on our seat backs. We circled the Circus Airport three times at full power before reaching 2,000 feet. Then we headed to the practice area on the other side of the city. By the time we reached 2,500 feet, we had been airborne ten minutes. My ears were ringing and my head was pounding from the noise.

"Level off," I yelled.

Dave reduced the power but anything less than 25 inches of manifold pressure and 2500 rpm produced a descent.

Our plan had been to review all of the exercises on the Private Pilot Flight Test. It didn't take long. The Lake's lack of performance simplified everything. Dave had been holding the best rate of climb speed throughout our climbs, descents and turns so we had already covered exercises one to eleven. That left stalls, circuits, forced approaches and navigation.

We had done a briefing on stalls. When we were ready, Dave moved the prop lever to full fine and reduced the manifold pressure with the throttle. With less thrust from the high-mounted engine, the Lake pitched its nose up. The airspeed dropped. The airplane started to descend. Dave raised the nose further. The gear-up horn sounded and the descent increased. Dave pulled the control wheel all the way back. The Lake stayed in a nose up attitude. It was rock solid. There was no buffet, pitch or wing drop. The rate of descent was the only clue that we were stalled.

"It won't stall!" Dave yelled over the blaring horn.

I pointed to the vertical speed indicator. It read 1,500 feet per minute, down.

"Oh!" Dave exclaimed.

He pitched the nose down. Whiskey's ears and jowls floated up in momentary zero gravity. The rate of descent pegged at 2,000 feet per minute. Dave added power. The nose tucked down further. The new windshield was filled with green fields and no sky. Our ten minutes worth of altitude was gone. Dave pulled back on the control wheel and leveled off. I wondered if donut-filled bloodhounds got airsick.

"Shall I do another one?" Dave asked.

I shook my head back and forth. "There aren't enough hours in the day to climb back up," I replied. "Let's go to the airport and fly some circuits."

"Good stuff," he said. The Lake's brick-like performance had not dampened his enthusiasm.

We approached the airport at 1,000 feet. "Simulate a forced approach," I yelled. "When you think you're close enough to the runway to glide from this altitude, cut the power."

"Okay."

On the base leg, the air traffic controller cleared us for a stop and go landing with a backtrack in between. Dave was a quick study. He continued in cruise flight with the power on. When he turned on the final leg a mile back, we were still at 1,000 feet. The beginning of the runway disappeared under the low sloping nose of the airplane. I looked at Dave.

"I can't miss with this baby," he said with a grin.

"I can't miss with this baby," he said with a grin.

We were too high and tight to make the runway with any other airplane. Dave cut the power. The nose pitched up, the speed dropped and the "gear up" horn blared. He pushed the nose down until we were pointed at the beginning of the runway and lowered the landing gear. From outside, it must have look like we had been shot.

"Everything okay there, Delta Uniform Delta?" the controller asked.

Dave punched the microphone button on his control wheel. "Just fine," he replied. Then he said to me, "I'm going to win every spot landing contest I can find with this thing!"

Dave held enough airspeed to allow him to flare out without power. As soon as he pulled the nose up, the Lake dropped on the runway - on the numbers. We were stopped before the 1,000-foot mark.

While taxiing back to the beginning of the runway, I said, "Let's try a short field takeoff: half flap and full power before brake release."

"Okay."

Dave extended the flaps and applied full fine pitch and maximum power. He looked at me. I gave him the nod. He released the brakes. The roar of the engine promised thrust that it didn't deliver. The Lake accelerated as quickly as a three-legged horse.

At the 2,500-foot mark, all three wheels were still on the ground.

"Pull back harder!" I barked.

"I am!" Dave yelled in reply.

At 3,000 feet down the runway, I was ready to call an abort when the nosewheel started to rise.

"Remember, don't let it come up too high!" I yelled.

I looked at the airspeed. We were going slower at this point of the takeoff than before but we were lifting off at the same distance along the runway. One thousand feet later we were airborne but the Lake refused to climb. The end of the runway flashed by. I reached over and selected the landing gear lever "up". The "gear up" light came on just as we scraped over the fence.

"Hey, that was better," Dave yelled enthusiastically. "I'll turn a bit to miss the trees," he offered.

"Good idea," I yelled in reply.

We didn't bother to climb to 1,000 feet to circle around for the landing. I told Dave to ask the controller for a full stop.

"Try a short field landing with full flap," I said.

"Okay."

On the base leg, Dave reduced the power. The nose pitched up and the speed dropped. He lowered the flap, extended the landing gear and dropped the nose. He had to reapply nearly full power to make it to the runway. We crossed the edge of the asphalt at less than five feet up. Dave cut the power. The nose pitched up and the airplane dropped on the numbers. Dave pulled the control wheel back and applied the brakes. We stopped by the 1,000-foot mark.

"That's great!" Dave boomed.

It was great if he could land on a 1,000-foot runway where the airport would build him another 4,000 feet for the takeoff.

"Taxi in," I said. "We have one more thing to do before we fly up north for water landings."

"What's that?"

"You'll see."

We parked on The Flying Circus ramp and shut down. Dave hauled Whiskey over the edge of the Lake's doorsill. I pushed the whale into the hangar. In the office, I went to the closet and pulled out our cargo scales while Leanne filled in Dave's bill. One of the requirements for The Flying Circus charter licence was to have a baggage scale. Ours came from Henry and Leanne's bathroom.

"What's that for?" Dave asked. He was already suspicious.

"I have a theory about why the Tooth Ferry's performance is so marginal," I said. I placed the scale on the floor and climbed on. "Two hundred and five pounds. Now you said that you weighed 235. With a 1700-pound empty weight, three quarters fuel at 180 pounds and 80 pounds for the dog that would put the Lake at a gross weight of 2,400 pounds. The airplane should perform better than it does. How about checking your weight?"

"Well I might be a little more," he said. He stepped back to distance himself from the scales. "But I was planning to start a diet."

"Me too," I said. "I'll challenge you. I'll bet that I can lose more weight in a month than you can but to start the contest, you have to get on the scales."

"What's the bet?" he asked with a chuckle.

"I don't know," I said. "We'll think of something."

"I belong to the Rotary Club," Dave offered. "The loser goes in the dunk tank at the Rotary Charity Fair next month."

"You're on," I said extending my hand.

Dave stepped forward and shook my hand. "We'll start with today's weight," I said. I held his handshake and tried to pull him to the scale. He wouldn't budge. With his free hand he reached down and picked the scale up.

"We'll let Leanne be the official judge," he said with a grin, "on the condition that she doesn't tell anyone the numbers."

He walked around the end of the flight desk, placed the scale beside Leanne's chair and climbed on. Leanne bent down to read the number. When she came up, her eyes were a lot bigger.

"Remember," Dave said to her, "this is our secret."

"How much, Leanne?" I asked.

"I can't tell you," she answered firmly.

"That's my girl," Dave boomed.

"Well, the number must have been under 300 pounds," I declared. Leanne gave me a negative stare.

"Just as I thought," I said, "over 300 pounds. When you said 235, you meant 335. The dog probably goes 100 more pounds and the aircraft empty weight is out-of-date. We've been flying the Lake well over gross. I'll book you a trip up north for next week to finish your checkout but in the meantime it's carrots, cabbage and water for you and Whiskey."

"Whiskey and I don't like carrots," Dave said in a wounded voice.

"That's even better. Just chew them for a while and then spit them out."

"Whiskey and I don't like carrots," Dave said in a wounded voice.

Chapter Nineteen

SECOND CLASS

The first booking for Barry McDay's instructor flight test was rained out. We needed him to instruct right away so we took the next available slot. It was the day Melville and I planned to work on the tractor.

I was going to cancel with Melville and go to The Flying Circus but Henry talked me out of it. "You'll be stuck here all day just to hear the ten-minute briefing at the end. I can do that for you. Besides, you know he'll do fine. Take the day off."

I took his advice.

Kevin Donaldson, the chief flight training inspector for the region, showed up to do the test. He spent the morning playing dumb student while Barry briefed him on several sample lessons. After lunch, they flew the Cessna 172 with Donaldson acting as the ham-handed student in the left seat. Afterward, they sat down with Henry over a coffee for a debriefing. Donaldson said that Barry had passed and had done an excellent flight test. He went on to congratulate Henry on the job we had done with Barry's course.

"If Mr. McDay is an indication of the pilots you are turning out here, you and your partner should be proud of this school," Donaldson said.

"Thank you, sir," Henry replied.

Donaldson pulled out his pad of temporary licences to write Barry an instructor's rating. "I'm not surprised, of course," he continued. "A couple of experienced Class One Instructors like you two should be doing a good job but you have my congratulations anyway."

"Thank you again," Henry said and then hesitated. "Neither of us are Class One Instructors. We are both Class Twos."

Donaldson frowned and looked at Barry's flight test application. My name and licence number was on the bottom as the recommending instructor. It said, "Class Two."

124

"I could have sworn you guys had been around long enough to be Class Ones," Donaldson said. "Surely you have enough instructing hours to qualify."

"Yes sir, we do," Henry said, blushing a little. "We've been so busy setting up this school that we haven't taken the time to test for the Class One. I was going to do it the next time my Class Two was due for renewal."

"I understand," Donaldson said. "Well I appreciate having two dedicated instructors in my region who turn out good pilots and don't generate complaints."

"Thank you, sir," Henry replied.

Donaldson wrote out a temporary Class Four Instructor Rating for Barry and then turned to Henry.

"Let me see your Instructor's Rating Certificate," Donaldson said.

"Pardon me?" Henry said.

"I want to see your Rating Renewal card," the older man said.

Henry pulled out his wallet, dug out his Rating Card and handed it to Donaldson.

He looked at it. "Class Two, you're right."

He wrote up a Class One Instructor Rating upgrade on the card, signed it and passed it to Henry.

"That's for a job well done," Donaldson said. He stood up, stowed his pen inside his suit and stuck out his hand to Henry and then Barry. "Congratulations to the both of you," he said. "Keep up the good work."

"Thank you," Henry said again, then he added. "My partner will be pleased to hear your kind words."

"Yes, well tell him anytime he books a flight test, his good work will surely net him a Class One Rating. Thanks for the coffee."

"You're welcome."

Henry phoned me with the good news that Barry had passed. He didn't mention his upgrade until I was back at work the next day. "By the way," he said casually, "when Donaldson was here, he gave me a Class One Instructor's Rating."

"He did two flight tests in one day?"

"Not exactly. He did one flight test and two Ratings."

What Henry was telling me was so unlikely that it wasn't sinking in.

"I don't understand."

"It's simple. Donaldson was so impressed with our operation that he thought we were Class One Instructors already. When I told him we weren't, he upgraded my card."

"I don't believe you."

He pulled out his wallet and showed me his new Rating. It meant that Henry had joined the elite few flying instructors in the country who were qualified to teach all levels of pilot licences and ratings. It also meant that he did not have to re-qualify for three years.

"Now the obvious question," I said. "What did he say about a Class One Instructor Rating for me?"

Henry smiled sheepishly, "He said anytime you book a flight test, your good work will net you a Class One Rating too."

"You're not serious."

"Absolutely."

I walked over to the telephone, called the Flight Training Standards office and booked myself a Class One Flight Test. I half expected Henry to stop me mid-dialing but he didn't.

"This isn't fair, you know," I said to Henry when I got off the phone. "You get a Class One over a coffee and I have to do a flight test."

"You're right," he replied, "but I wasn't about to point that out to Donaldson when he was here and risk having to do a flight test myself."

"It still isn't fair."

He smiled and put his hand on my shoulder. "I'd offer to do your flight test for you but you'd fail."

My flight test was in two weeks. I meant to study. Class One candidates were required, "to demonstrate an above average standard of instruction in all levels of licencing." That translated into, "the inspector could ask you to teach him anything about flight training and you had better be good."

A couple of evenings at home I fell asleep on the chesterfield with the instructor book in my lap. Susan woke me up to go to bed. "Why don't you take a day off and study?" she asked.

"We're too busy," I replied. "Besides, according to Henry, the flight test is a formality. I'll get the Class One based on my good record."

The big day arrived and with it Inspector Kennedy, my nemesis.

He was dressed like an undertaker but didn't smile as much. He was a hard, miserable man who specialized in bringing out the

I meant to study.

worst in flight test candidates. I had endured several flights with this man and during each one I had done something stupid to lower his opinion of me. I had gotten lost on a Class Two Instructor ride and shut down the good engine on my initial Multi-Engine Rating flight test.

When he walked through our door, I wanted to blurt out, "Where's Inspector Donaldson?" but I knew it wouldn't do any good. I pretended to be pleased to see him. He didn't return the favor.

"Good morning sir," I said, offering my hand. "Thank you for coming."

"You should know that the department personnel cannot afford the time to conduct unnecessary flight tests," he declared with a scowl chiseled into his face. He ignored my outstretched hand.

"This is a Class One upgrade ride, sir," I said hopefully.

"Everyone waits until their Class Two is due for renewal before attempting this test," Kennedy said.

127

"My mistake, sir," I replied, but I didn't offer to postpone it for a year. I should have. "Would you like a coffee, sir?"

"No, I don't drink coffee. It's unhealthy," he declared. "Do you realize that there are only 63 Class One Instructors in the country right now?

"No, sir, I did not know that." He was telling me that he did not agree with the way his boss was handing out Class One Instructor Ratings like good-behavior badges. I knew then that I was wasting my time taking this test. More importantly to him, I was wasting his time.

"Over 50 of those Class One Instructors are government inspectors," he added.

He pompous attitude was bugging me. "All good people, I'm sure," I said, "like yourself, sir."

"And the rest of them," he continued as if I hadn't spoken, "have applications into the government to become inspectors."

"Well sir, we might as well see if I'm qualified to join such an illustrious group. What would you like me to teach first?"

"Give me the pre-flight briefing for the dual cross-country," Kennedy said. "Assume that I have not taken any ground school classes."

He had just sentenced me to three hours of hard work. I bit my tongue to squeeze the sarcasm from my voice and dug in. I outlined the route and the objectives of the lesson. Every time I tried to move along, Kennedy stopped me with a technical question.

"What does Transverse Mercator mean?"

"It's the type of projection that was used to represent a round globe on a flat piece of paper."

"Explain the differences between that projection and the ones used on other aeronautical charts."

"As a Private Pilot student, you don't have to know that, sir," I said. I tried to inject respect into my reply but it didn't come out.

"Right, but as a Class One Instructor, you do, so explain it to me."

When I asked him to do some of the planning like a student, he said, "You show me."

The three hours stretched into four.

During a break for lunch, Kennedy sat in his government K car. I ate my bologna sandwich in the office and fumed. "The man is a career assassin," I muttered to Leanne. "What happened to the concept of public servants?"

"Oh, I'm sure he's just doing his job," she replied hopefully.

"Right. He's promoting aviation safety," I said. "The safest pilot is the one on the ground without a licence."

Kennedy came back in and we finished the crosscountry briefing.

"Now brief me on the first lesson on instrument flying." I thought I detected smugness in his voice but it didn't show on his granite face. "You can assume that I haven't read the textbook," he added.

Kennedy made me explain the function of each instrument in the cockpit. When I reached the gyro attitude indicator, he asked what caused acceleration error.

"It's only a problem on fighter jets being catapulted off aircraft carriers," I said. I was unable to keep the exasperation out of my voice.

"Some of your students will go on to fly high-performance aircraft," he snapped back. "Do you know the explanation or not?"

I launched into the complicated gyro theory as best I could remember it from when I first learned to instruct. I sounded rusty. Kennedy made me teach it all.

We went flying in one of the Cherokee 140s. Kennedy told me to teach a short field takeoff over an obstacle followed by a departure on the crosscountry that I had planned.

"Assume this is my first time and demonstrate each lesson," he said gruffly.

I let his miserable attitude affect my flying. I did a slam, bang, bad job. Twenty minutes into the crosscountry, he pulled the throttle to idle. "Show me how you teach a simulated forced approach."

There was nothing below but a sea of fruit trees. I pushed the throttle back in. "I would do some safety checks before starting the lesson," I said, looking around for an open field.

Kennedy pulled the power back. "Show me what you would do if your engine really failed right here."

I flew an approach to a farm lane between the trees. I would have made it but it would have been tight. The airplane would have been damaged. Kennedy reapplied the power at 500 feet above ground.

Kennedy reefed the Cherokee into a series of left and right steep climbing turns.

"I have control," he barked. "Put the hood on."

"I don't wear the hood when I'm instructing," I said firmly, "the student does." I held the hood out for him to wear.

He kept both hands on the controls. "I want to see if you can fly the airplane on instruments from the right seat for when you run into bad weather with a student. Wear the hood!"

I slipped the hood over my head. While I was doing that, Kennedy reefed the Cherokee into a series of left and right steep climbing turns trying to induce vertigo. "You have control," he yelled a few seconds later.

I had taught unusual attitude recoveries from less violent

manoeuvers so I knew what to look for but my return to a normal climb involved some initial over-controlling. Kennedy then covered half the flight instruments with rubber suction cups and asked me to turn to a specific heading in the climb using only an altimeter, turn coordinator, airspeed indicator and compass. None of this tested my ability to teach. He was just making me angry.

We covered most of the Commercial Pilot Course. He made me do all the talking and the flying. We finished up with a short field landing demonstration back at the airport. I slammed the airplane on the runway, dumped the flaps and hauled on the brakes. It was short but not very sweet.

If I was being marked for my attitude, then I was probably going to lose my pilot licence. The best I could hope for was being busted back to a Class Four Instructor which meant that I would lose my Chief Flying Instructor and Flight Test Examiner status.

I shut down the airplane, climbed out and followed Kennedy into the office. He didn't say a word. We took a table on the far side of the room.

"Well," he said, pulling out his licence pad. "I didn't see any improvement over your last Class Two flight test so I'm not going to give you a Class One. Just so we didn't waste our time, I'll renew your Class Two. That will give you two years to hone those instructing and flying skills."

"Thank you, thir," I said through clenched teeth. It was a lie. I wasn't thankful at all.

Kennedy completed the paperwork. "I understand your partner is a Class One Instructor," he said.

"Yes thir, he is.

"Well maybe he'll spend some time giving you some pointers before that next flight test."

Chapter Twenty

EAVESDROPPING AND SUMMER SAULTING

Leanne worked at The Flying Circus from nine o'clock until four, Monday to Friday. Her schedule minimized the impact on her pre-teen children, Victor and Gretchen. She saw them off to school, came to work and was home again when they returned. The only difference was that the housework wasn't done. The kids didn't care.

We hired Eavesdroppers Answering Service to take our phone calls when there was nobody in the office. Myrtle Knickenbacher, Barney Swallow's sister-in-law, was Eavesdroppers' owner and sole employee. She was perfect for the job. Over the phone, she sounded like a perky 30-year-old. Henry and I went to her house to meet her. We were greeted by a tall, thin 50-year-old in pink slippers and a purple housecoat. Her hair was out of control and she had the odd habit of spitting drool when she talked. The house wasn't exactly dirty but there were piles of magazines and newspapers everywhere. On top of the piles were telephones, one for each of her customers. A few rang during our visit. She waited four to six rings before answering them.

"The number of rings is up to the customer," she explained.

The sweet voice didn't fit the body but she seemed efficient. At Myrtle's request we gave her copies of our promotional handouts so she could learn our business. She asked questions about what we did and when we worked. She explained, while showering us with bits of drool, that she had three objectives when answering our line: be helpful, make the caller think she is at the airport and never lie. We weren't sure what she meant but we signed the contract and left to escape the spittle.

After we were hooked up with Myrtle, Al Milton, Henry's laugh-a-minute student, called one day to change a booking. Leanne had gone home and there was no one in the office.

"Good afternoon, The Flying Circus," Myrtle said sweetly.

Al was surprised by the strange voice. "Who's this?" he asked.

"It's Myrtle Knickenbacher. How can I help you today?"

"You must be new," Milton replied. "Ah, is Leanne there?"

"No, I'm afraid she has left for the day. I can have her call you tomorrow."

"No, that's all right. Is Henry there?"

133

"No, I believe he's still up flying. Can I have him call you as soon as he comes in?"

"I need to reschedule my booking tomorrow," Al said.

"I'll let Henry know that you're canceling for tomorrow," Myrtle replied. "Do you have another time in mind?"

"Is he available Friday at two o'clock?"

"As far as I know he is, but I'll have him confirm it with you. What is your name and phone number?"

Al gave her the information and then asked, "Is this an answering service?"

"I work at reception, answering calls, making bookings and helping the customers however I can. Is there anything else I can do for you Mr. Milton?"

"No, thank you," he said. He liked the voice. "Maybe we'll meet the next time I'm at the airport."

"I hope we do."

We backed up Myrtle at her game. I was the next one to pick up our messages that day. I returned Al's call to confirm his booking.

"Who's the new babe working the desk?" he asked.

"Oh, that's Myrtle."

"Myrtle?"

"Yah, Myrtle Knickenbacher, why do you ask?"

"She sounded too good for you guys. How do you con these women to work for you?"

"Like flies," I replied with a laugh. "They hang around this office and incessantly beg Henry and me for a job just to be near us."

"Right. In your wildest dreams," he chuckled. "When I see her, I'll tell her that she's working for a couple of losers."

"You're just jealous. You're confirmed for two o'clock on Friday. I'll give Myrtle your love."

Al came in for his next lesson looking for Myrtle. Leanne was working the desk.

"When does this Myrtle girl work?" Al asked casually.

"She helps out when I'm not here," Leanne replied.

"Where did you find her?"

"She's related to the airport manager. She's a nice girl."

"She sounds nice," Al agreed. "When do I get to meet her?"

"Her hours are hit and miss. Did you want me to give her a message?"

"No," Al laughed, "I'd rather give it to her myself."

She leaped to the other side of the flight desk.

On Friday that week, Barry's sister, Summer, took her introductory flying lesson with Ray Tragunno. When they returned, Leanne had gone home for the day.

"Damn, there's nobody here," Ray cursed. "I don't see how these guys expect to make any money if they don't have the staff to collect it."

"The invoice is right here," Summer said, looking at the flight

135

desk, "and I have money on an account. My brother is paying for my first lesson."

"That's good," Ray replied, "but we need someone to book our next flight. I'm available on Sunday and Monday."

She leaped to the other side of the flight desk. "I'll have a look."

"I'll catch the washroom," Ray said.

Summer figured out the reservation sheets and booked a lesson for herself with Ray on Monday. Then she entered the flying time on the invoice and the daily log using the previous entries as a pattern.

Al Milton walked in from a flight with Henry who was still outside turning the airplane around. Summer looked up with her bright blue eyes and flashed him a friendly smile. "Hi," she said cheerfully.

"You must be Myrtle," Al replied, closing the door.

She didn't know who he was talking about but it didn't slow her down. "And you must be the Flim Flam man," Summer replied.

"You know me pretty well already," Al laughed.

He leaned over the counter and offered a handshake. "I'm Al Milton," he said.

Summer stood up and gave his hand a full athletic squeeze. "Pleased to meet you," she replied.

"Likewise," Al winced. He looked at his compressed fingers. Henry walked in.

"I don't understand how this guy gets pretty girls like you to work for him," Al said with a laugh.

"I'm in his custody," Summer replied with a smile. "He signs me out on a work pass from the Women's Correctional Facility."

Al didn't expect such a bold-faced reply from this innocent-looking girl. For the first time at The Flying Circus, he was lost for words. Henry didn't have a clue about what they were saying.

"Mrs. Rains has started your bill," Summer said to Henry. "I'll fill it in for you if you tell me how long you were."

"One point four hours," Henry said without jumping into the rest of the conversation.

Summer turned to Al. "I see you're charging to your account, Mr. Milton. Would you like to make another booking?"

"Al, call me Al," he said. He was still struggling for words. "What are you serving time for?"

"Embezzling," Summer replied without hesitation, "but it won't happen again. I'm studying accounting so I won't get caught next time. Can I put you down for another lesson?"

Al had met his match.

Ray came out of the washroom. "Hi Al, how's it going?"

"Ah, fine, fine."

Ray turned to Summer. "I gotta run. When do I see you next?"

"Monday," Summer replied, "at two o'clock."

"Fine, I'll be here," Ray said. "Catch you later," he said to Henry.

"Thanks for coming in, Ray."

After Ray had left, Al said, "I'd like a booking on Monday too, if Henry's available."

"Sure," she replied, looking at the flight sheets. "What time?"

"Two o'clock."

"Two o'clock with Mr. Rains is fine."

The next two days were busy. It was a good weather weekend at The Flying Circus. Barry and I split it with Henry and Ray. Barry and I worked Saturday and they covered Sunday. We spent most of the time flying, staying in the office only long enough to check messages with Myrtle, return calls and sign out our next flight. By the end of the weekend the office was a mess. No one had cleaned up and the invoices for all the flying activity were piled high.

Leanne came in on Monday to a dirty office and a pile of paperwork. She had spent the weekend cleaning up at home but she plowed into it anyway. She spent the whole day alternating between cleaning and accounting. The bright spot in her afternoon was meeting Summer McDay. The university student came early for her lesson hoping to talk to Leanne. Her timing was perfect.

"Hi Mrs. Rains. I'm Summer McDay, Barry's sister," she said in her best, bright-eyed and cheerful greeting.

"Oh, yes," Leanne replied with a smile. "Call me Leanne," she said standing up to shake Summer's hand. "I'm pleased to meet you."

Summer was smart enough not to crush her fingers.

"You're the girl who stumped Al Milton last week," Leanne continued. "Henry told me about it. Nobody had done that before."

Summer blushed. "He seemed like the kind of guy who was good for it. I hope I was right."

"Oh sure," Leanne replied. "If you can't have fun like that, why breathe."

"I agree but I've been known to go too far."

"Don't worry about it here. Does Ray still think you're named 'Summer Salts'?"

"Yes," she blushed again. "That one went over his head."

"Most things do," Leanne laughed knowingly.

"I assume it was you who completed the invoice for your last flight. I wanted to thank you. It was the only one done right over the last two days."

"You're welcome. I noticed that you don't have anyone working the flight desk when you're not here. My university courses leave me extra time. I have experience working with the public. I wonder if you would be interested in my covering some of it for you?"

"I would but our income hasn't caught up to our expenses. We can't afford anyone right now."

"I'm really enjoying the flying. Would you trade lessons for the desk work?"

A grin of relief slowly spread across Leanne's face. The prospect of sharing the desk load was suddenly within her reach. "Yes, I certainly would. When are you available?"

"Every Saturday, Sunday afternoons and one evening a week."

"You're on!" The smile spread.

"That's great," Summer exclaimed. "I'll do my best not to joke too much with the customers."

"I'll be disappointed if you do. People are supposed to be coming here to have fun," Leanne said. "I'll show you some reception-ist's things now until Ray is finished flying with the student that is ahead of you, if that's all right."

"That's why I came early."

Summer walked behind the desk and they sat down to work.

A half-hour later, Al Milton came in for a lesson with Henry followed by Ray and his student.

"Hello Myrtle, hello Leanne," Al said. "Am I interrupting something?"

"Al, this isn't Myrtle," Leanne said. "Her name is Summer McDay. She's going to be working the desk part-time."

"We met on Friday but she said her name was Myrtle."

Ray stepped into the conversation. "Her name is 'Summer', Al,

Summer Salts. She was flying with me on Fri. . . ."

Ray finally connected on the trick name. "Did you say 'McDay'?" he asked Leanne.

"As in Barry McDay," Leanne replied. Summer smiled.

"You mean I've been hitting on Barry's wife?"

Summer immediately realized that if she was Barry's wife, Ray might be less interested in her and more interested in teaching her to fly. She didn't correct him. "No harm done, Ray," she said.

"I thought your name was Myrtle," Al said to Summer.

"Who's Myrtle?" Summer asked.

"Myrtle answers the phone when I'm not here," Leanne said.

"What else don't I know about you?" Ray asked Summer.

"Yah," Al said, echoing the thought. "Are you really out on a . . . , you know, a prison program?"

"Sure," Summer said mischievously. "It's called 'university'."

At that point, Barry McDay walked in. Summer walked over and gave him a big hug. "Hello darling," she said.

He backed up in surprise, "Summer, get off me," he exclaimed. "What are you doing?"

"Yup, they're married all right," Al said. "When do we get to meet Myrtle?" he said to Leanne.

As soon as he had said the words, Henry walked through the door with Myrtle. She had asked him for an introductory flying lesson and they had just flown it. The purple housecoat, pink slippers and unruly hair were replaced with a crisp tent dress belted at the waist, pink sandals and a slightly lopsided blond wig.

Leanne spoke first. "Al," she said, "meet, Myrtle Knickenbacher. Myrtle, this is one of our favorite customers, Al Milton."

"Mr. Milton," she said in her regular sweet voice, "I'm pleased to meet you. We've spoken on the phone."

I was afraid of how Al would react. He was expecting Marilyn Monroe and he was meeting Phyllis Diller. He proved that he could be a perfect gentleman given the right occasion. This was the right occasion.

"Myrtle, it's a pleasure to meet you. Have you been flying?"

"Yes, we just came down and I've never had so much fun in all my life."

"That's great," Al replied. "And you're the lady who answers the phone when Leanne isn't here."

"Yes, that's right."

"Well, can you tell me how Henry and his partner manage to find such good looking women to work for them?"

In the middle of all the noise, the telephone rang. Summer answered it. "Good afternoon. This is a flying circus."

Chapter Twenty-one

GREASING THE AXEL

George Heinkle opened our office door, looked at me and announced, "There vill a customer be."

"Good morning, George," I said.

George's English was literally translated from German. It took more than one sentence to catch what he meant but eventually it came out.

Henry and I didn't see George very often or for very long. He came when we called about the shared capital costs on the Cessna 172 that he leased to us. He conducted the meetings with one hand on the open door. He would listen, respond, nod his head and leave.

Today was different. No one had called him. He continued into the office and closed the door.

"This customer vill be a relative of my vife visiting from Germany."

"When does he arrive, George?"

"He is at my house a guest now. He vill come here this afternoon."

"Good, what can we do for him?"

"He vants to fly my Cessna."

"Okay," I said. "Does he have a pilot licence?"

"From Germany."

"All right, we will take good care of him."

"No! He is to be treated like a common person even vhen he mentions my name. He must be checked out like everyone else."

"Okay, George, I think I understand. How is his English?"

"He speaks four languages but he does not listen to any. You have to know that Axel is my vife's brother's son."

"Your nephew," I replied.

"My vife's nephew," George corrected. "You must also understand that most Germans are nice people."

"I believe that," I said cautiously.

"Axel is not von of them," George continued. "I vant you to not think my family is like this boy."

"Okay," I said agreeably. George frowned. "I mean, yes, I will not think that," I added quickly.

"Axel vill be difficult. He deserves nothing but please take his costs from my lease payments on the Cessna."

With that, he nodded his head, turned on his heels and marched to the door. With one hand on the knob, he turned and said, "Thank you. I think you vould say that this von I vill owe you." He opened the door and was gone.

That afternoon I was getting ready to fly with a student when a grey Porsche convertible screamed into our parking lot and slid sideways to a stop. The male driver and female passenger jumped out laughing. They were blond and in their early 20s. They hopped onto our steps and stormed through the office door.

The boy looked at Leanne, stopped smiling and turned to me. He flexed his facial muscles into a sneer and said, "My Uncle George says you vill give me his plane, ya?"

"You must be Axel," I said extending my hand in greeting. He looked at it like I was handing him a dog turd. He clasped his hands behind his back.

"I vould appreciate you give it to me now, ya?" he said.

"Well," I replied in a strained friendly tone, "I would be happy to schedule a check out for you tomorrow. You will need a visitor's pilot licence from the government before you fly the airplane yourself. Did you bring your logbook with you?"

"Look," he said with forced patience, "I don't tink you understand. I have been in za planes before. Dhere is notting to flew dhem. You give me za airplane now and Ursula and I go for a ride."

His girlfriend leaned back to show off her tight leather pants. She was chewing a large wad of gum.

"Before you can have the airplane," I answered, trying to sound tough, "you will have to fly with an instructor. I can book a lesson for you tomorrow morning..."

He held up his hand and shook his head as a signal for me to stop talking. He lifted his chin and looked down his nose at me. "Listen. I don't have za time to teach your instructors," he said forcefully. "I go flying now vit Ursula!"

I tried a new tact. "Tell me Axel, would you loan me $25,000

He shook his head as a signal for me to stop talking.

right now? My wife and I need it for the afternoon but I'll give it back to you at the end of the day."

"Vhat is dhis nonsense talking?" he demanded. The veins in his neck and head were swelling.

"Well, you want me to loan you a $25,000 airplane. We have never met. I'd like some reasonable expectation of getting it back in one piece. You will have to fly with an instructor - tomorrow."

"Za plane is not yours," he said loudly. "It belongs to mine uncle. You vill give it to me now!"

Before I could answer, Leanne spoke up. "Henry is available as soon as he comes down," she said, enunciating clearly. "I know he would be pleased to fly with Axel right away."

I didn't want to bother Henry with this guy. I wanted to prove that I could handle him but Leanne was using a hard-edged voice that I had never heard before. She smiled at me through clenched teeth. "I think I hear him taxiing in now," she added.

The look on her face told me to back off, so I did. "Mrs. Rains will take care of you," I said to the sneering youngster.

"Very vell," he replied.

I turned to my waiting student and started a pre-flight briefing. I was only half paying attention to what I was doing because I was more interested in what Leanne had in mind.

Axel stood with a scowl on his face and his arms folded until Henry walked through the door. Leanne spoke first. "Henry, this is Axel, George Heinkle's nephew visiting from Germany." I didn't see it, but there must have been some secret signal between Henry and his wife.

"From Germany!" Henry exclaimed with exaggerated enthusiasm. "That must be your Porsche parked outside. That is a fantastic car." Cars were the least important things in Henry's life. He drove an old, rusting, flesh-colored Ford Pinto.

Axel kept his arms folded. He flexed his sneer without saying anything. Henry was smart enough to not offer a handshake.

"Axel would like to fly his uncle's airplane," Leanne explained.

"It is a pleasure to met someone related to George," Henry said. "I would be happy to take you flying."

"I have already from Germany za pilot licence. You give me mine uncle's plane." His accent was thick. His tone was flat and threatening. "I fly myself vit Ursula."

"Your English is very good," Henry said. It was a lie. "Is this your first visit to Canada?"

"Vhat does dhat matter?" Axel replied angrily.

"You need a Canadian pilot licence. Otherwise we have no insurance coverage for you," Henry said calmly.

"I fly lots in Germany," Axel declared. "German pilots are za best in za world. You give me za plane."

"Leanne can arrange a visiting pilot licence for you but it will take a couple of days. In the meantime, we could take Ursula along, fly over Niagara Falls and you could show Ursula and me what a good pilot you are."

I could see that Axel wanted to explode but he was measuring the firm but friendly stance in Henry's voice. Before he could say anything, Henry continued. "I have never flown with a German pilot,"

Henry said. "I bet you could teach me a few things."

"I did not come all za vay here to teach you flying," Axel said. "I don't have much time."

Henry walked over to Ursula. He helped himself to her handshake even though it wasn't offered. "Ursula, I'm Henry Rains. It is a great day for flying. Can you talk Axel into taking us up?"

It is possible that she did not understand English. Axel barked at her in German. She smiled nervously through her chewing gum but did not speak.

"Very vell," Axel said to Henry, "ve go flying." His tone was softening a little.

"Let's go then," Henry said, taking the Cessna logbook offered by Leanne. "I'll help you pull the airplane out and check it over." I heard Henry speak before he closed the office door behind him. "I've always wanted a Porsche."

When I was done briefing my student, I sent him to check the airplane over while I signed us out.

"I hope you didn't mind my intervention on that one," Leanne said a little nervously. "I could see Axel was trouble and I knew that Henry had lots of experience with that type."

"Don't worry about it," I said. "I must say that I've never seen Henry like that before."

"Henry's father-in-law is an aging Axel," she continued.

It took me a few seconds to connect to what she was saying. "You mean your father acts like Axel?"

"Brigadier General Horatio Montgomery, the same. When the army spends your whole life telling you how great you are, you believe it. I find Dad intolerable. Henry has him eating out of his hand."

"I don't know how he can take it."

"Me either."

"Well, he's welcome to it."

"That's what I thought."

When I landed an hour later, Henry was still up with Axel and Ursula. They came in after I was finished with my student. The three of them were laughing together like old friends.

"Leanne," Henry said with an exaggerated chuckle, "you should have seen the look on Ursula's face when Axel did a steep turn over Niagara Falls. I thought she was going to jump out of the airplane."

Axel grinned proudly. He translated what was said into German

145

for Ursula and then laughed uproariously. It was Ursula's cue to laugh too. She did. Leanne dutifully smiled.

"Of course the turn was flawless," Henry continued. "There was never any danger."

Axel translated. Ursula nodded knowingly. "I'm sorry that we couldn't do stalls, spins or forced approaches," Henry said to Axel, "but you know how the regulations are with passengers on board. If you are available any time this week, we'll go up again."

"Ya, any time," Axel said obligingly.

"And I want you to meet this friend of mine with the grass strip. You won't believe this place until you see it."

"Ya, I vould like dhat."

I could tell that Henry was manufacturing excuses to fly more with Axel. Obviously he had made friends with the surly German but Axel must be a lousy pilot. They made another booking. Axel thanked Henry for the flight, ignored Leanne and me and left with Ursula.

"Congratulations," I said to Henry, "you have made friends with the Fourth Reich."

Henry smiled, but only slightly. "My dog could fly better and she can't reach the rudder pedals."

"Leanne," I said, "Check the insurance on the Cessna before he sends the Luftwaffe solo in it."

"I already have."

Chapter Twenty-two

GLENN VS MARGARET

The Hathaways' new airplane was ready. The Piper Aircraft distributor in Toronto was delivering it on Thursday. This was a big event at The Flying Circus. The Hathaways had talked about "their new baby" freely and frequently to any flying school customer who would listen. They had visited the factory in Vero Beach, Florida while their Archer was being built. The Piper people had given them a tour of the assembly line and allowed them to sign their names in grease pencil inside the airframe before it was closed up. I could imagine Margaret wanting to shake hands and talk to every worker in the plant. They took pictures and when they got back, showed them around the flying school.

Long before the big day, Summer had offered to help organize social events.

"What social events?" I had asked. Henry and I had been working long days. We were not in a "social" mode.

"Oh, I don't know," she said. "At the church we have regular bake sales, card nights, dances or teas. The events make you feel closer to the rest of the congregation."

Al Milton was there. He didn't hesitate to speak up, as always. "You're talking over their heads, Summer," he said with a chuckle. "They have trouble knowing who they are when they get up in the morning. I'd help you with a barbecue."

"A barbecue is a great idea." Summer replied enthusiastically. "The church has a big grill we could borrow. A barbecue would give our customers a social reason to come out to the airport."

Leanne jumped into the conversation. "Why don't we plan a barbecue around an open house for the flying school. We could schedule it to coincide with the delivery of Margaret and Glenn's new airplane."

It was a nice idea but it wasn't my way of running the business. I talked to Henry about it in the privacy of the hangar. "I just hate to tie up a good flying Saturday with a social event," I moaned.

"Maybe we could do it in the winter when we won't lose so much revenue from flying time."

"I know what you're saying but when have you been to a Christmas barbecue?" Before I could answer, he continued. "Everyone has been working long and hard. Maybe it's time to give ourselves a break. Think of it as a chance to stop and appreciate what we've accomplished."

"You've got a point," I admitted. "How about an evening barbecue? We could shut down the flying early."

"We're making money flying with our current customers but if we neglect promotions like an open house, where do the next ones come from?"

"If we get more new customers, we'll have trouble flying with them. Saturday is one of our best days."

"Let's look at it another way," Henry said patiently. "On a good Saturday we can fly 12 hours with the three airplanes. Right?"

"Right."

"That helps us pay some bills and maybe come out with a $4-an-hour profit. That's $48, right?"

"I'm listening."

"If we take time out to entertain our customers and show them a new airplane, we might interest someone else in buying one."

"That's true but the important thing is to keep our airplanes flying. That $48 a day profit is why we're here," I said. "Hopefully it will double and keep on doubling."

"I think to grow, the flying school has to offer more than just flying," Henry persisted. "For instance, it took two phone calls to arrange the purchase of the Hathaway's Archer. For that, the Piper distributor is paying us $1,500."

I hadn't known what we were making on that deal. "I think the barbecue/open house is a great idea," I quickly declared.

Leanne talked to the Hathaways. They readily agreed to display their new Archer on the Saturday following delivery. Leanne placed advertising in the "Personal" column of the newspaper.

Al Milton, who was an inspector for the Department of Health, said he would donate the steaks. "Will they be rejects?" I asked, just to give him a hard time.

"Don't knock it," he replied seriously. "Meat aged beyond the government maximum can make the best steaks you ever tasted."

I wasn't sure if he was saying "yes" or "no".

PERSONALS

• If you ever dreamed of learning to FLY, come to the FLYING CIRCUS Barbecue/Open House @ the airport this Saturday info: FLY-4FUN (359-4386)

Summer arranged to borrow the grill from the church. "I've already talked to my choir mates about coming to the open house. This is a great chance to get friends interested in flying."

She and Leanne published a newsletter inviting our customers to come and see the new airplane. Bruce Stanwick said he would donate homemade grape juice from his farm.

"I'll bring donuts," Dave Michelin announced.

"You're on a diet," I reminded him.

"The ones with the holes," he countered.

To pacify me, Henry booked Barry and Ray to fly sightseeing flights and introductory flying lessons during the open house. That left the other Cherokee 140 and the Hathaway Archer for a static display.

Two days before the open house, the new airplane was delivered. Margaret and Glenn were there when it was flown in by the distributor, Buzz Billings. A few customers and most of the staff were also on hand. The airplane looked great. It was mostly white with two colored stripes along the sides. Piper changed the shape of the

149

stripes from year to year but that seemed to be the limit of the company's imagination. Margaret had chosen a red stripe and Glenn picked gold. After some negotiation, Piper had agreed to paint the stripes on one side gold and red, and red and gold on the other.

Billings taxied the Archer onto our ramp and shut it down. I had never met the man but he was exactly what I had imagined an aircraft distributor would be like.

"Howdy folks."

Billings popped the door open on the right side, hoisted himself across the seats and climbed onto the wingwalk. "Anyone here looking for a new airplane?"

He was a short, round man with balding hair and a chubby, tanned face. Billings was dressed in Piper colors: bright red sports jacket, white shirt, sky blue pants and white shoes. He should have had a cigar in his mouth to complete the picture of a true salesman.

He shook a meaty hand with all of us and then opened the baggage door and engine cowling for the Hathaways to inspect their new purchase.

The registration on the airplane was the most fun. The Canadian government aircraft database had arbitrarily assigned "C-GVMH". When Glenn saw the red letters painted on the tail, his face split into a huge grin. "Glenn versus Margaret Hathaway," he declared laughing. "It's perfect."

"Oh, Glenn," Margaret protested.

Having witnessed the opposite ways that the couple flew, Glenn's interpretation of the registration was accurate.

Henry had finished the paperwork for the sale and registration of the aircraft so the only thing left to complete the delivery was a checkout for the new owners.

"Buzz," I said to the smiling salesman, "I'd like to ride in the back seat when you fly a checkout with the Hathaways. I'll be flying with them during their instrument training."

The salesman's smile dropped considerably. He looked at his watch. "I wasn't planning on any checkouts," he announced. "Cherokees are Cherokees. If you've flown one, you've flown them all," he said to no one in particular. Then he turned to me. "You take them up and you'll all be fine. Now, who's going to fly me home?"

"I was going to fly you home after the checkouts," I persisted.

"Well, good buddy," he said, placing his hand on my arm and giving me a fake smile, "I don't have time to give rides. Delivery includes bringing the airplane here and getting a lift back, not checkouts. I'll leave you and these fine folks to enjoy the new airplane and I'll scoot on out of here. Who've you got to give me a ride?" He made a point of looking at his watch again and then at Henry.

This guy was bugging me and Henry could tell. He continued looking at the engine in the new airplane and stayed out of my conversation.

What bothered me was that Billings had just made an easy $5,000 profit for flying an airplane from Florida to Toronto to Circus. Henry had done the selling and the paperwork. I thought Billings should do more than just grin for five minutes and then disappear.

"If the Hathaways agree," I said, "we'll fly you to Toronto in their airplane. That way, they'll get their checkouts and you'll get your ride."

"That's fine with us," Margaret and Glenn said at the same time.

Billings set a pained expression on his face. "Well, I was counting on a quick trip back." He looked at his watch again. "A first flight in a new type of airplane isn't the fastest way to go anywhere."

"Nonsense," I said. I put my hand on his arm just like he had done to me. "Cherokees are Cherokees, once you've flown one, you've flown them all. We'll have you there in no time."

I didn't wait for his reply. I turned to Glenn and Margaret. "I'll let you two decide who's going to fly first. We can switch for the flight back."

"Margaret can go first," Glenn said.

"Glenn can go first," Margaret said at the same time.

"Ladies first," Glenn said, breaking the tie.

"Okay, then," I said before Margaret could protest, "Margaret, you climb into the left seat and familiarize yourself with the cockpit and Glenn and I will do the walkaround inspection."

"I did a walkaround before coming here," Billings said.

"Good," I replied. "Let us know if we miss anything."

"I'll sign you out on the flight sheets," Leanne volunteered. "Do you need charts?"

"Yes, please," I replied.

"I'll get a tow bar," Henry offered.

We all got to work except Billings who stepped out of the way. To his credit, he seemed resigned to accept the slow ride home.

It was a treat to see an airplane without a scratch, dent or stain on it anywhere. When we had done the pre-flight inspection and turned the airplane around, Glenn climbed onto the wingwalk and into the back seat. Billings gestered for me to follow.

"No, it's okay, Buzz," I said with my hand on his arm again. "Margaret and I have flown Cherokees before. We'll be fine. Climb in."

He started to say something and then decided against it. He joined Glenn in the back seat. I climbed in and sat down beside Margaret. The interior had that wonderful "new car" smell. Margaret was rummaging around in her handbag. I held the door ajar for fresh air while she pulled out a tissue and tucked it up the right sleeve of her sweater.

She turned and smiled at Billings. "In case a girl gets the sniffles," she explained.

152

I was familiar with Margaret's pre-flight routine but I could imagine the aircraft salesman doing a slow burn behind me. He didn't say anything.

Margaret reached into her purse again and extracted a tube of lipstick and a compact mirror. She turned to Billings. "It's part of my pre-start check," she said with a bigger smile.

"Take your time," he said. His tone was impatient.

Margaret finished applying the lipstick, dropped the tube back into her purse and dug out a bag of scotch mints. She held them toward the back seat. "Candy?" she offered.

I turned to look at Billings. He was fit-to-be-tied. "No thank you," he said through clenched teeth.

Margaret also saw his look. "I'll be ready to go in a minute," she said.

There was a checklist in the aircraft side pocket but Margaret pulled her own Cherokee 140 list from the purse. She held it up.

"Will this one be all right?" she asked Billings.

"Sure," he replied automatically.

I had been looking around the cockpit. Billings had been right. Most of the knobs, levers and dials were similar to our smaller flying school airplanes. They were just newer. Piper had done its homework to make moving up to an Archer easy.

Margaret started running through the checklist rapidly and out loud. In a matter of seconds she was done the pre-start check. She pumped the throttle, yelled "Clear!" out the pilot's side vent window and turned the key. The engine fired, chugged and then settled into a smooth, throaty idle. She turned off the electric fuel pump, checked the engine gauges and called the ground controller.

"Good afternoon, Circus ground. This is Golf Victor Mike Hotel requesting taxi instructions for a VFR flight to Toronto." She released the microphone button. "It's hard to say that registration the first time."

"Good afternoon Mrs. Hathaway," the controller replied. "The new airplane looks great. The runway is 24, wind 240 at 20 knots, altimeter 2992; you're cleared to taxi Charlie, Bravo to hold short of 24, call the tower for takeoff."

"Thank you," Margaret replied, "Runway 24, Victor Mike Hotel." She turned and smiled at Billings again. "The boys in the control tower here are very friendly."

She released the brakes, gunned the engine and taxied the airplane at a fast clip. She pulled up beside the runway and immediately started into a pre-takeoff check. "Seat belts on," she said to everyone. "Door closed," she said to me. Without waiting for a reply, she spun the radio selector to the tower frequency and called for a takeoff clearance.

"Victor Mike Hotel is now cleared for takeoff Runway 24, wind two four zero at twelve."

"Victor Mike Hotel."

I just got the door closed and latched in time as Margaret accelerated onto the runway. She continued into the take-off roll all in one motion. I could feel the extra pull of the 180-horsepower engine. Her face was split with a wide grin. "This is great!"

The extra torque that came with the power pulled the Archer to the left. Margaret corrected onto the centreline before I had to say anything. I thought she might hold the airplane on the runway for one of her patented "zoom" climbs but she behaved herself and pulled back on the control wheel as soon as the airplane was ready to fly. The Archer eagerly lifted off.

She turned to me and whooped, "I love the power!"

"It makes a difference," I replied.

We crossed the far end of the runway passing through 300 feet. The airplane climbed easily despite the full load. The engine was loud but in a deep, satisfying way. I daydreamed a few seconds inside the wall of noise and thought how nice it would be to have a new airplane like this for the school. The dream was shattered by a sudden silence. The engine quit. There had been no warning, no burp or sputter. The propeller was windmilling but the engine was dead.

Margaret and I exchanged "What did you do?" looks. I pushed forward on the control wheel.

"I have control!" I announced in a loud voice.

My actions were automatic and deliberate. I had many hours practising engine failures after takeoff with student pilots. I pointed the nose down, set up a glide and turned slightly left. I knew that the Dairydale Dairy sewage lagoons were straight off the end of the runway. I headed for the evaporation field beside the lagoons.

There was nothing automatic or deliberate about what was going through my mind. It was racing to figure out what had killed the engine. I had about 10 seconds before this brand new airplane would be landing across the ditch-filled evaporation field. I could feel Billings pulling on the back of my seat to lean forward. He didn't say anything. Nobody said anything.

I glanced down. The fuel selector was on "left", the tank was three quarters full, the ignition was on "both", electric fuel pump was "on", throttle was "full", mixture was at "rich" and the fuel primer was locked. I selected carburetor heat "on" although I didn't expect that ice was a problem on this balmy summer day.

One hundred feet to go.

"I'm going to land in this field," I said loudly, pointing left of the ponds. "Seat belts tight, everybody; eyeglasses off."

I traded hands on the control wheel long enough to reach up and unlatch the door at the top. I should have warned my passengers. The door popped with a load bang followed by the "swoosh" of wind blowing passed the crack. Margaret let out a short scream which failed to drown out the noise of a startled Billings cracking his head against the roof.

I concentrated on the landing. I searched vainly for the smoothest section in the long grass. It all looked the same from that low altitude but I knew that there were ditches in the field. Just above the ground, I raised the nose and lowered the flaps with the lever between the seats to slow down. I continued to pull the nose up. The stall warning horn sounded. I held the control wheel all the way back. The Archer flopped into the field. I stood on the brakes. The left main tire dropped into a hidden ditch almost immediately and sheared off. The left wing dug into the ground. The airplane slewed left. I pushed full right rudder. We bounced and banged our way across the field. It sounded like we were inside a steel drum being rolled through a stone quarry. Out of the corner of my eye I could see grass, mud and milk being thrown up from the left wing.

Milk!

We were still travelling at a good clip when the nose gear dropped into the next ditch and broke off. The nose plunged into the ground. We were thrown against our shoulder harnesses. The door flew open. The windshield turned white. The tail came up as the airplane plowed to a stop.

The silence was sudden. I looked around. The cabin had remained intact. I started to breathe out a sigh of relief when I was thrown hard against the instrument panel and pinned there. Billings had rammed the back of my seat forward. He reached for the doorsill and propelled himself through the small space between my seat and the doorway.

155

I pushed myself back. "Everyone okay?" I asked. I became aware of milk dripping on my head from the top of the door opening.

"I think I'm all right," Margaret said.

"Okay, back here," Glenn said.

"Good. Let's get out in case there's a fire."

I undid my seat belt and climbed onto the slanted milk-covered wingwalk.

"You go first," Glenn and Margaret both said at the same time.

It was not a good time for discussion. "You're next Margaret," I declared, firmly.

She slid across the cockpit and I helped her onto the wing. The airplane rested on its crumpled left wing and curled propeller. The tail and right wing were high in the air.

I jumped down off the back of the wing to make room for Glenn to climb out. I landed in four inches of sour milk. The dairy used the evaporation field to dispose of stale product. It was shallow enough that it didn't show through the long grass but deep enough to flow into my shoes.

I reached for Margaret. "I'm fine," she said.

"I'll help you anyway," I said. "What you don't know is that I'm standing in milk." As I said it, a putrid smell wafted up from my feet. I picked her up from the wing and then swung my left arm under her legs. "Go off the front of the wing, Glenn," I said. "It'll be easier."

"Okay," he said.

The next thing that wafted up from my feet was a swarm of mosquitoes. The milk-laden field was an ideal breeding ground for the blood-thirsty insects. Since I was carrying Margaret, there was nothing I could do about them except move. I squished and slogged my way toward Billings who was standing on a ridge of dirt at the edge of the field. Glenn followed us. The mosquitoes swarmed into my hair and on my bare arms. Margaret did her best to wave her free hand around without losing her grip around my neck.

Billing's high ground was a line of overgrown dirt piled from a ditch dug along the edge of a field. The ditch was on the other side of the ridge. It was full of sour milk. We climbed onto the dry mound beside him. He didn't offer to help. I put Margaret down.

"You were pilot-in-command," Billings said, madly swatting mosquitoes off his bald head. I knew he was referring to whose

156

157

insurance coverage he thought was going to pay for this one.

"Somebody said that the delivery is not complete until the distributor gets a ride home," I countered. "That means it's still your airplane."

"I'll see you in court," he said.

"Okay," I replied, sounding more confident than I felt. I planted my feet firmly on the mound, shoved him in the chest and sent him flying backward into the ditch of sour milk; red blazer, blue pants, white shoes and all.

Chapter Twenty-three

AFTER THE CRASH

The three of us hotfooted it along the uneven ridge as fast as we could, vainly swatting at the swarms of mosquitoes. We were outnumbered. Buzz Billings hauled himself from the milk ditch and charged after us. We came to a farm track that bridged the ditch, cut through a line of trees and crossed a hay field to the county road. As we turned to follow it, I looked back at the wreck sitting cock-eyed in the middle of the field. Our landing had left a trail of flattened grass and broken irrigation pipes.

"Don't worry about it," Glenn said, reading my mind. "We walked away."

"Thanks, but I feel badly about trashing your new airplane," I said.

He put his hand on my shoulder, "Forget it. Piper can make us another one."

Buzz brushed passed us on the run. "You'll hear from my lawyer," he sputtered. The cloud of bugs around his milk-soaked clothes was the thickest. We followed him along the dirt path. By the time we reached the road, we had been bitten on every piece of exposed skin.

We could hear the sirens of emergency vehicles in the distance. The air traffic controller had watched us go down. He had called the local fire, ambulance and police numbers. Multiple vehicles were dispatched from each of these departments, no doubt with thoughts of a large airplane disaster. The emergency convoy, sirens blaring and lights flashing, started arriving as we came to the county road. The fire chief was the first to reach us. He couldn't see the airplane.

"Are these all of the survivors so far?" he demanded.

"These are all of the people involved," I said.

"Where is the crash site?"

"Along this dirt road, through those trees and in the middle of the next field."

"Okay," he bellowed, pointing at me, "you come and show us the location."

"The survivors are mine," a paramedic yelled, jumping out of an ambulance. "You folks come with me," he said motioning us toward his van.

"Hey chief," a policeman shouted over the din of still more arriving sirens, "my captain wants to know if you want to call out the army reserve?"

"Hell, no!" he yelled back. "Not yet." Without saying anything further to me, he climbed into the nearest truck and led a charge of fire vehicles, police cars and ambulances along the farm road.

"Who has the worst injuries?" the paramedic demanded of our group.

"None of us is injured," I answered.

"You're okay, how about you ma'am?"

"I'm fine," Margaret said.

Vehicles continued to arrive, clogging the country road. The paramedic asked Glenn and Buzz if they were okay. Then he wasn't sure what to do next.

"It was a small plane," I explained. "There are only four of us. We're okay. Thanks for coming."

A newspaper reporter shoved a tape recorder microphone under my nose. "It was a small plane and only four survivors?" he asked.

"It was a small plane and there were only four of us," I said clearly. "We're all okay."

"No casualties?" He sounded disappointed.

"Well, I lost a lot of blood to the mosquitoes," I offered.

Henry arrived and rescued us from further interrogation. "Everybody okay?" he asked.

"Yes," I said.

"Good, let's get out of here."

While the reporter was heading down the dirt track and the paramedic was explaining what little he knew to his coworkers, the five of us walked past the blockade of emergency vehicles to Henry's Pinto parked down the road.

"There isn't room for all of us," I said. "I'll stay and see what I can do here until you come back."

"Okay," Henry said.

I walked back through the knot of cars and trucks until I was stopped by a policeman. "I'm sorry sir, this area is sealed off. You'll have to stay on the other side of the road."

The adrenaline rush from the crash was starting to wear off. I

160

thought that I should be doing something but I felt suddenly tired. "Sure thing, officer," I replied.

I joined the line of onlookers who had parked their cars on the far shoulder. Since the wrecked airplane was behind the trees in the next field, they could only stare curiously at the melee of emergency vehicles.

The one-lane farm track was creating a bottleneck of flashing lights. New emergency vehicles arrived, turned down the dirt road and blocked the departure of the ones in the field. I stood quietly for half an hour while the police officers sorted it out. Most of the onlookers had left by the time the bulk of the emergency vehicles departed.

"You're a member of a flying circus?"

When there were just a few police remaining at the end of the farm road, I walked up to one of them and introduced myself as the pilot of the subject aircraft.

"We've been looking all over for you," he declared.

161

"Well, it took me a while to get clear of the paramedics," I lied. "I assume you'd like a name of someone responsible for the wreck."

"Certainly. So you're the owner?" the cop asked, flipping open his notebook.

"No, I'm just the pilot. The airplane is owned by Buzz Billings Distributors in Toronto. I work for The Flying Circus here at the Circus Airport."

"You're a member of a flying circus?"

"Yes, I am," I said without explaining that it wasn't a circus to be a member of.

"And you were the pilot of the airplane that crashed?"

"Yes, sir."

"What company do you work for?"

"The Flying Circus," I replied.

"Yes, I got that," the policeman said, "but what company do you work for?"

I handed him a business card. "It's all on here," I said.

Henry pulled up in his Pinto. He nodded a greeting to the policeman and spoke to me. "I arranged for Barry to fly Buzz back to Toronto. I talked to the accident investigator. He's not coming until the morning. He will be instructing the police to post a guard on the airplane until then. If this officer is done with you, we might as well go back to the flying school."

The policeman said he was done. Henry and I got in his car and he drove to the office. "I feel badly about the Hathaways," I said on the way. "That airplane meant a lot to them."

Henry pulled a small roll of one hundred-dollar bills from his pocket and placed it on the seat between us. "Not as much as their lives," he said. "Glenn gave me $500 before they headed home. He said it was an extra 'thanks' for how you handled the emergency. I told him it was your job but he insisted."

"He didn't have to do that." I felt embarrassed.

"No, he didn't but it's funny how people appreciate it when you save their lives."

"Well, I still feel badly. Everyone put a lot into organizing the open house barbecue and now we'll have to cancel it."

"I don't think so," Henry said. "In fact, this little incident will put The Flying Circus on the map for a lot of local people. I asked Leanne to place a display ad in tomorrow's newspaper inviting the

162

public to view the wreck during our open house on Saturday."

"You what!"

"I think when people see the news coverage of the crash, they'll be curious. I'm expecting a large crowd."

I thought Henry had lost his mind. "But airplane crashes are bad news," I said. "Why display a wreck for the public?"

"People associate airplane crashes with death and destruction. This is an opportunity to show them that a landing in a field is routine."

I couldn't see how inviting the public to view a wreck was going to encourage them to fly but at that point, I couldn't argue. I was too tired.

Henry knew what I was thinking. "Don't worry about it."

Chapter Twenty-four

BACK ON THE HORSE

"Hi, Honey, I'm fine."

"What's wrong?" Susan asked.

She was on an overnight trip visiting the stores in her territory. I called Susan every night when she was away.

"How do you know anything is wrong?"

"You never call me 'Honey' unless you want something such as 'to start a flying school' or when you break something. Normally when two people telephone each other, they ask, 'How are you?' The 'I'm fine' part comes second. So what did you break?"

"The Hathaway's new airplane."

"But you're fine."

"Yes, and so are they but their Archer is a write-off."

"What happened?"

"The engine quit on takeoff and I tore the airplane up landing it in Dairydale's milk pond."

"Well, I'm glad you're okay. I'm sorry I'm not there for you. I bet you're in a bit of a knot over that one."

She was right but I hadn't realized that I was until she said it. "No, I'm fine," I lied.

"What are you doing tomorrow?"

"Henry and I meet with the accident investigator in the morning, then we start taking the airplane apart."

"Go to the airport early and go flying."

It was the last thing I expected her to say. "I think I've had enough flying for now," I replied.

"When you fall off, you get back on the horse. Believe me, it works. Do a couple of circuits. You'll feel better."

"I'll see if I have time."

"Make time, it'll be worth it. But do me a favor."

"What's that?"

"Pick an airplane with an engine that doesn't quit."

"Okay. Will I still see you Saturday night?"

"Yes. I'll bring wine and we can toast gravity."

"You're on."

I didn't sleep much that night. I replayed the takeoff in my mind over and over. I tried unsuccessfully to find some clue to the engine failure. The next morning I went flying as Susan had suggested. It made me feel a little better until I spotted the wreck off the end of the runway. I did one circuit and landed.

Henry brought the morning Circus Chronicle with him. The headlines read, "Mosquitoes bleed crash survivors." Underneath was a picture of the four of us being examined by the paramedic. Under that was a photo of the wreck in the field. Coverage of the accident included a statement from Leanne. "Flying Circus office manager Leanne Rains said that the company will continue with plans for an open house tomorrow. 'If the accident investigators have finished with it in time,' Mrs. Rains said, 'we will have the crashed aircraft on display. We want the public to see that flying is safe even when an off-airport landing is necessary.'"

The story continued, "Accident investigators are expected on the scene today. They are hoping to find what caused the airplane's mysterious loss of power."

It took Pierre less than five minutes to find the cause of the engine failure.

165

Investigator Pierre Savoir met Henry and me at the office at eight
o'clock. The short, trim man had the firm handshake and brush-cut
hair of a former air force pilot. He seemed friendly and easygoing.
He listened to my description of the brief flight and then asked for
photocopies of the last few pages of the aircraft logbook.

"It's routine procedure," he explained.

"There is only one page," I said. "It was a brand new airplane."

I copied the Journey Log page and handed it to him.

"Thank you. Are you guys coming with me to the scene?"

"Yes, if that's okay with you," Henry said.

"Certainly but you'll have to drive your own car. Mine is full of
the tools of the trade," he said. "I'll follow you since you know
where it is. I take it we are headed for a bug infested swamp."

"Worse," I replied, "but how did you know? Is my face still that
swollen?"

"No, you're wearing rubber boots and insect repellant. It's not
normal attire for a flying instructor."

"Would you like some?" I asked, pulling a bottle of bug lotion
from my pocket.

"No thanks," he said. "I have my own in the car."

We followed Pierre out to the parking lot and waited while he
retrieved boots and repellant from the back of his government station wagon. We could see that the "tools of his trade" included all-
weather clothing, rope, camera equipment, shovels and cutting
gear.

We drove around to the other side of the airport. There was a
policeman guarding a barricade at the entrance to the dirt road leading to the wreck. Pierre showed his credentials and arranged for the
two cars to drive in. We parked on the bridge at the edge of the
field. Pierre stepped out of his car and looked at the layer of milk
at the base of the grass. "I should have brought my cat," he said
with a smile. "He would have liked this."

He pulled on his rubber boots. Henry and I walked with him to
the airplane. It took Pierre less than five minutes to find the cause
of the engine failure. He lifted off the front cowling, looked around
the engine compartment and pointed to the braided fuel hose that
was supposed to be connected to the carburetor. It was sticking
straight up.

"It won't run like that," he said and then looked at me. "You were
lucky there was no fire. With both fuel pumps running on takeoff,

there would have been gas pouring out of here just above the exhaust."

"What would have caused that to come off?" Henry asked.

"Nothing if it had been put on right," Pierre said. "The airplane might have come from the factory with the hose on finger-tight and it took this long to vibrate off."

He took a picture, picked up the cowling and placed it over the engine. "I'm done. You can tell your insurance company that I have released the wreck."

"There's a little problem with that," Henry said as we headed back to the cars. "It could be Buzz Billing's insurance company or ours. I talked to both of them yesterday and there is some dispute over who should cover the flight."

"Well, I'll leave it to you," Pierre said. "I'll tell the cop that I have released the airplane. As soon as I do that, he will leave and you'll be on your own."

"Thanks, Pierre," Henry said as we reached his car. He shook our hands.

"Good luck."

Henry and I went back to the airplane and took the radios out. They were the most expensive, easiest to remove parts. Then we headed back to the office in his car. It was 08:30.

"It's going to be hard getting that thing out of the swamp," I said on the way.

"I know," Henry replied. "I'll call Darcy at Derry Air and ask him to bring his flatbed trailer down, help us take the wings off and haul the wreck to the hangar until the insurance gets settled."

"Okay," I said. "I'll gather up some tools and put them in your car. We might as well get started taking the wings off."

"It's not going to be fun working in four inches of sour milk."

Henry turned his Pinto onto the airport entrance road. We found The Flying Circus parking lot plugged with three big hydro trucks, one with a trailer and backhoe attached. We parked on the side of the road and walked to the office. Inside, the lounge was crammed with orange-suited hydro workers and their foreman Bruce Stanwick. Leanne was serving them coffee.

"Hi there," Bruce said. "I heard you guys were playing in milk. We were on our way to a job and thought you might want a hand."

"Hi, Bruce," I said. "The investigator has released the airplane but we haven't even started to take the wings off yet."

167

"Do you want the wreck in the hangar?"

"That's the idea," Henry said.

"Well, if you give us a few minutes, we could do that with the wings still on."

His reply was a signal to his men. They got up, thanked Leanne for the coffee, put their boots on and headed for their rigs. Henry looked puzzled.

"He means it," I said knowingly. "Let's go."

We followed the men out the door. Bruce jumped into the truck pulling the backhoe. Henry and I climbed back into the Pinto. Henry turned it around and led the convoy to the crash site. When we turned down the county road that ran past the wreck, the crew in the last truck stopped and set up a roadblock. A flagman directed traffic to the next road. The men in the second truck did the same thing at the next intersection.

When Bruce reached the farm path, he backed his rig and trailer all the way to the bridge. Henry and I followed in Henry's car. We watched as the crew unloaded the backhoe. Its front-end loader was fitted with two long wire spool spikes. The operator drove across the field, slid the spool spikes under the wreck, lifted it out of the milk, drove slowly back to the bridge and gently placed in onto the trailer.

Henry's face split into a huge grin. "Come on," I said. "Let's get our car out of their way."

Bruce followed us in the hydro truck pulling the trailer. He stayed in the middle of the path with the Archer's wings sticking out each side. The backhoe was being driven behind him. The whole entourage turned left and headed to the entrance side of the airport. When we reached the main road, the hydro crew had it barricaded. The flagman was talking to the drivers of the first cars being held up. Henry and I scooted ahead so we could pull the airplanes out of the hangar to make room for the wreck. By the time we had the three airplanes out, the hydro truck and trailer pulled up to the opening. The backhoe operator picked up the wreck, carried it into the corner of the hangar and placed it on a set of sawhorses that Henry set up. Then he drove his rig back onto the trailer.

It was nine o'clock.

"Well, I'll see you at the barbecue tomorrow," Bruce said to Henry and me.

"I don't know how to thank you," Henry said. "You saved us at least a full day's work and a lot of expense."

"Happy to help," Bruce replied with his shy smile.

"Tell your men they're welcome to join us for a steak-on-a-bun tomorrow," I said.

"Okay, I will." With that he swung into the hydro truck cab and drove off.

Chapter Twenty-five

HENRY AND SPLASH

The open house was a hit. The public saw the headlines and responded to our newspaper invitation. They came in droves to gawk at the wreck. By ten o'clock, our parking lot was full. By eleven, cars lined both sides of the airport entrance road. Henry and I manned the hangar. I stood by the bent Archer and talked to a steady stream of curious people. Then I passed them to Henry. He sat them in the shined-up Cherokee that we had parked beside the wreck. We didn't let them get away without taking handout sheets on sightseeing flights and flying lessons.

The weather was sunny and warm so Leanne closed the office and set up a table and chair in the entrance to the hangar. She sold airplane rides and introductory flying lessons. Business was brisk. Barry McDay and Ray Tragunno were busy flying all day. Al Milton cooked steaks with help from Summer McDay. They set up an empty coffee can with a hand-lettered sign on it, "Steak-on-a-bun and grape juice - $5 - all proceeds to charity". Al had brought a hundred steaks. I told him it was too many.

"Then I hope you like beef," he replied and then chuckled. "I've inspected the plant where these came from and you won't catch me eating them."

Dave Michelin brought a party box of donuts, mostly cream filled. Leanne set him up beside her with the coffee maker. His coffee can sign said, "Coffee and donut - $1 - pet the dog - 25 cents - jokes - free - proceeds to charity".

"When you land a wheelplane in a milk pond, do you log that as a seaplane flight or a breakfast flight?" he asked me and then roared.

Dave spent the whole day eating Bavarian creams and spouting one-liners. "Tell me," I heard him ask one little boy who was petting Whiskey, "are people who eat Corn Flakes for breakfast called cereal killers?

"Do you call people who stop smoking 'quitters'?" he asked one

Leanne sold sightseeing flights. She kept Barry busy flying the Cessna all day.

couple who paid for a joke.

"Can I have my money back?" the man asked.

"No, but I'll give you two for one if you can tell me why the turtle crossed the road."

"I don't know," the man replied.

"To get to the Shell station," Dave said. "You owe me 50 cents."

Bruce Stanwick came with several of his hydro workers and their families. I thanked them again for saving us from a day of laying in bug-infested sour milk to take the wings off the wreck. I told Al and Summer that The Flying Circus would pay for steaks for the hydro crew. Al told me afterward that Bruce had tossed a fifty-dollar bill in the donation can.

171

"That's not right," I said. "He's done too much for us already."

Al laughed it off. "Don't worry," he said. "If I had his money, I would throw mine away."

The busy day helped me a lot. I was still bothered by the crash. It was nice to know that the engine quit due to a mechanical failure but I mentally replayed the short flight trying to think how I might have handled it differently. Working with the public all day took my mind off it.

They were the most unlikely looking learn-to-fly candidates

During the afternoon, Summer introduced Henry and I to three friends from her church choir. They were the most unlikely looking learn-to-fly candidates but I thought it was nice that they had dropped by for the barbecue. They were the long, the short and the small. Reimie was a gangly six-footer. She was shy but her size and booming voice made it impossible for her to go unnoticed. Hilda was older, rounder and a lot shorter. Kate was a thin and quiet librarian type.

"It was nice of you to drop by," I said, shaking their hands as they were introduced to Henry and me.

"I'll arrange for Summer's brother Barry to take the three of you on an introductory flying lesson," Henry said. "He's flying the Cessna 172. You could go together."

The three girls were wallflowers. I knew Henry was wasting his breath.

They exchanged shy glances. Kate blushed deeply. Hilda spoke up. "We'd like that," she said.

You could have knocked me over with a feather.

"Good," Henry replied. "Come on over and meet my wife, Leanne. She'll fit you into the schedule."

And so it went. At the end of the day, Barry and Ray had flown nearly 40 introductory lessons and sightseeing flights. Leanne booked several more for the next few days. Ten people had signed up for flying lessons, including Summer's three church-going wall-flower friends. Al was out of steaks and Dave had eaten or sold all the donuts but was still telling jokes.

"Have you met Henry and Splash? They own The Flying Circus."

Chapter Twenty-six

BUZZ JOB

" It was a good thing that we picked up more customers at the open house," Leanne said. "The bank raised its prime interest rate another full percentage point. That puts the mortgage on the hangar at eleven and a half per cent."

"What does that do to our payments?" I asked.

"The two per cent rise over the last two months has added nearly $1,000 to our monthly interest."

"Can we pay it?"

"So far, so good, but I was hoping to get ahead before the fall when business will drop off. Every time we get more customers, our bank payments wipe out the extra income."

"I appreciate your doing the bookkeeping, Leanne. Henry and I would have lost track of it long ago."

"I know," she said and then smiled. "I like doing it. It's a nice change from housework."

"Well, the interest rates can't keep going up."

"I hope you're right."

The new customers kept us all busy, too busy to worry much about the bank payments.

The week after the crash, an adjuster from the insurance company covering the Hathaway Archer came to The Flying Circus office. Russ Landsdowne was a middle-aged, medium-sized businessman. He talked to Henry, the Hathaways and me in a pre-arranged meeting. Buzz Billing was to join us with his adjuster to settle the claims growing out of the accident.

"According to our lawyers, the delivery of the aircraft to the new owners and the signing of the paperwork legally constituted the change of ownership," he explained. When he spoke, I felt we were listening to a friend. "Since both of these things had been accomplished prior to the crash, my company will be covering for the accident. We don't have a problem with that," he continued. "That is what insurance is for."

174

Then he turned to the Hathaways. "The bad news is that your policy contains a $1,000 deductible on the hull damage," he said softly, "and your insurance premium for the year gets wiped out by the accident. If you intend to buy a replacement airplane with the settlement, you would require another premium."

"Oh, that's fine," both Hathaways said at once.

"We're just glad no one was hurt," Glenn added.

"And we want to buy another airplane," Margaret said quickly.

"Well, that's the spirit," Russ replied. "When the others get here, I'll do the talking and we'll see if we can get some of your money back."

Buzz Billings arrived as planned with his insurance adjuster. Buzz talked. As Russ predicted, Buzz was adamant that the ownership changed when the airplane was delivered and the paperwork signed. It was obvious that he didn't want the claim on his insurance.

"A grey area has developed over your insistence on the day of the crash that the delivery was not over until you were returned to your home base," Russ said.

Buzz clinched his jaw and did not answer. Russ continued. "Does your insurance company know about your refusal to provide a check ride for anyone on the new aircraft?"

"Their licences are valid for any single-engine, piston-powered airplane," Buzz said. "A check ride was not legally required."

He was right, but Russ wanted the adjuster from Buzz's company to know what kind of operation he was running. He saved the best for the last.

"According to the logbook, your mechanic signed this airplane out as being airworthy less than an hour flying time before the crash. Are you interested in debating who is responsible for the fuel line being loose?"

"My mechanic never touched that fuel line," Buzz said with exaggerated anger. "His signature is based on the FAA certification that comes from the Piper factory. Talk to them."

Russ pulled out the Billings Enterprises' invoice for the Archer. "On here you've added $500 for 'pre-delivery inspection'. Are you still not responsible?"

"The pre-delivery inspection does not include fuel lines!" Buzz declared. By now, Buzz's face was red. The anger was not exaggerated. "When the airplane went down, your client owned it. If

175

Buzz knew he was being squeezed from both sides.

you're trying to duck coverage, you're not passing it to me."

"Well," Russ said slowly but firmly, "if my company pays for the accident, I'd like concessions from you in exchange for being kept out of it."

Buzz didn't say anything but he was listening.

"First of all, give the Hathaways a $500 refund for your non-inspection. Second, pay The Flying Circus $500 airfare for your flight back to Toronto that you now claim was not part of the delivery. Thirdly, order and deliver a replacement airplane to the Hathaways at your distributor price which I guess is $5,000 less than they paid for the first one."

"No way!" Buzz exclaimed. He stood up as if to leave. "Come on," he said to his insurance adjuster. "I don't have to listen to this nonsense."

His representative stayed in his seat and called his bluff. "Before you go Buzz, think about this," he said. "We've established that you no longer owned the airplane at the time of the crash. That means you did not have insurance coverage on it. If any liability is assessed on your company, you would be paying out of your own pocket."

"That's ridiculous," Buzz snapped. "I pay you for liability insurance."

"That covers airplanes that your shop worked on. You say your mechanic never touched it. You're on your own. Russ has made you a good offer. I'll add that if your company is proven liable, it may be grounds to terminate your insurance coverage."

"You're trying to blackmail me!" Buzz knew he was being squeezed from both sides. "Yours is not the only insurance company, you know."

"I know," his rep said, "but the insurance business is a small world. News of bad risk travels fast."

"Sit down, Buzz," Russ said smoothly. "This isn't going to cost you real money. Write me two cheques for $500. They will be coming out of profit on the first airplane that you didn't really earn and then order another airplane. I'll pay you for it right now, wholesale. We won't tell the government about your negligent inspection practices and Piper will think you are doing a great job selling their airplanes."

Buzz huffed and puffed some more but in the end he went for it. Russ's insurance company replaced the wrecked Archer for $5,000 less than the cost of the original. He was kind enough to bury the Hathaway's $1,000 deductible in his company's savings. The Hathaways received $500 from Buzz. So did The Flying Circus.

177

Chapter Twenty-seven

ONE MAN'S JUNK

After the insurance was settled on the Hallaway's bent Archer, Bruce Stanwick casually asked Henry and me what would happen to the wrecked airplane.

"It belongs to the insurance company now, Bruce," I said. "Normally they sell it to a salvage company. Why do you ask?"

"I'd like to buy an airplane when I finish my pilot course. It appeals to me to rebuild a wreck, especially if it saves money."

"It's not worth it, Bruce," I said. "The adjuster said it's a write-off. When the left wheel hit the ditch, the left wing got yanked hard enough to bend the spar box in the fuselage. The wing and fuselage are scrap."

"Well maybe we can find another wreck that was hit on the right side," Bruce offered.

I was about to suggest that it was a bad idea but Henry spoke first. "I'll talk to our mechanic, Darcy, and see what he says. In the meantime I'll tell the adjuster that you are interested."

"Thank you," Bruce said. "If we can put a deal together, I'd be interested in talking to you about leasing the airplane. Could you use an Archer in your fleet?"

My immediate thought was that we needed another airplane but an Archer would be the third type in a four-plane fleet. It wasn't a good idea.

"Yes," Henry said quickly. "With all that extra radio equipment and extra performance, it would make a good advanced trainer. It would also appeal to licenced pilots as a rental airplane."

They both looked at me to see what I had to say. I was thinking how all of Henry's decisions had worked out for us. "Yes," I said agreeably, "we need another airplane and it would be perfect for our fleet."

"She's toast," Darcy declared.

Darcy flew down from Derry Air later that week to look at the
wreck. Bruce, Henry and I were there.

"Hi Crash," he said to me as soon as he stepped out of the airplane. "So you found out a Cherokee glides like a cement mixer,
eh?"

"The accident investigator said it was a maintenance problem," I
replied.

"Can't trust those mechanics," he said. "Where's the trash?"

"It's in the hangar." Then I added, "This is Bruce Stanwick, the
fellow interested in it."

Darcy shook Bruce's hand. "Let's have a look," he said.

He walked around the Archer and then climbed into the cabin. He
pulled some tools from his pockets and was soon handing out the
seats and carpet.

He invited Bruce to climb on the wing and look inside. He pointed to the spar box. "She's toast," he declared, pointing at the bent
heavy-gauge aluminum. "You could buy another fuselage and left

179

wing but the labor costs to transfer everything else from here to the new pieces would add up to more than the cost of a new airplane."

Bruce had been watching him quietly. "If the spar box is not cracked, can a frame shop straighten it?" he asked.

"Like an automotive frame shop?"

"Yes."

"I don't think so. First of all, the only way to get the bent left wing off is to cut it, then you're stuck with the spar stub jammed in the bent spar box."

"What if we used the wrecked left wing in place to straighten the spar box? Once it was back in line, the wing should come off and a new one could be installed."

Darcy looked at Henry and I standing in front of the wing peering over the open door. He smiled. "I like this guy," he said. "He has a brain and he knows how to use it."

Bruce smiled.

"There is the outside chance that it might work if the spar box has not been bent too far. You have the problem of getting the airplane to a frame shop with the left wing still attached and then there is the question of jigs. Piper has the only Archer jigs that I know of. You'd need them to get the wings both going in the same direction."

"I work for Provincial Hydro," Bruce said quietly. "We get our share of twisted hydro trucks from tipovers. There is a shop in Derry that has a computerized laser frame machine."

"You're talking about Enzo Bigolo's place."

"That's right," Bruce replied.

"The man works magic with that machine," Darcy said. There was a growing excitement in his voice. "A friend of mine races stock cars on weekends," Darcy explained. "Enzo does all his frame work. He might be able to do it. His machine would measure the good side of the wreck," Darcy said, thinking out loud, "and the computer would flip the measurements and apply them to the left side. He doesn't use jigs."

"That's right," Bruce said.

"That's clever. It might work." He looked at Bruce. "Are you sure you're a pilot?"

Bruce smiled again.

"We should get Enzo down here to have a look at this," Darcy said.

"I did," Bruce replied. "He was here yesterday. He said no problem."

180

"Well then there's only finding a way of getting the wreck to Enzo's shop with the left wing on."

Henry and I looked at Bruce. He blushed. Henry answered for him.

"Trust me, Darcy," Henry said. "It's not a problem. But I wouldn't bet against hydro-induced traffic tie-ups between here and Derry on the day he does it."

Bruce smiled.

He spent another hour with Darcy making a list of the replacement parts that would be needed to rebuild the airplane. I went flying with a student and Henry called Russ Landsdowne. He explained that Bruce was ready to bid on the wrecked Archer.

"So far I've got two low bids from salvage companies and a higher one from Buzz Billings," Russ said.

"Billings? He doesn't do salvage."

"I suspect that he will order the replacement Archer as a 'green' airplane, transfer the interior and radios from the wreck and sell the rest to one of the salvage companies."

"That's good to know," Henry said. "You'll be receiving a bid from my man by the end of the week. Can you wait that long?"

"Sure, no problem. In fact, sometime this week I was thinking of taking some time off to go to the racetrack. I hear that horse Number 11 in the tenth is a sure thing."

Henry only hesitated for a moment. "Well, good luck. It was nice talking to you."

Henry told Bruce to bid $11,000 if he wanted to buy the wreck from the insurance company. He did. The next week he was the proud owner of a bent Archer.

Three familiar hydro trucks pulled into The Flying Circus a few days later. One was towing a trailer with the backhoe on it. Another trailed an empty flatbed. Twelve men got out including Bruce Stanwick. Three of them unloaded the backhoe while the rest attacked the broken Archer with electric screwdrivers. In 20 minutes they had removed the right wing and the horizontal stabilizer from the tail. The backhoe operator picked the rest of the wreck up and placed it on its right side on old tires covering the flatbed trailer. The bent left wing pointed skyward. They lashed it all down including the good right wing. The whole operation took 30 minutes. It was beautiful to watch.

"Do your guys want coffee?" I asked Bruce when they were finishing up.

He looked at his watch. "Are you making it?"

"No, I'll ask Leanne to make it."

"Okay then, a quick one. We have to drop this load off at Derry and be back in the Hydro yard by 4:30."

Chapter Twenty-eight

SPLASH DOWN

"How much weight have you lost?" I was talking to Dave Michelin on The Flying Circus ramp. It was time to teach him how to takeoff and land his Lake amphibian on water. We had planned to fly north to Dave's cottage for the lesson.

"I don't know," he answered with a chuckle. "I'm waiting for the end of the month to surprise myself."

"You've got jelly donut powder on your face," I said. It was true.

"Thank you," Dave replied, running his hand around his grin. "That's the best part." He licked his fingers.

Dave's insurance company required him to take ten hours of dual instruction on water flying before acting as pilot-in-command to his cottage. I had called his insurance agent to clarify what we should cover during the lessons.

"What exactly do you mean by 'water flying'?" I had asked.

"It's flights that take off and land on water," the agent replied.

"So if Dave and I fly from the Circus Airport to his cottage and back, it doesn't count as 'water flying' because we used the airport?"

"Will the flights take off and land on water?" he asked.

The guy was obviously reading from a book. I tried a different approach. "If we take off from water, fly for 10 hours and then land on water, does that meet your 'water flying' requirement?"

"Will the flights take off and land on water?"

He either knew nothing about flying or was being dumb as a fox and not committing to anything. I tried once more. "If we taxi around on water for 10 hours and during that time, become airborne momentarily, does that meet your requirement?"

"If the flights take off and land on water."

"Thank you."

"You're welcome," he had replied cheerfully. "Call anytime."

My biggest concern with the water work was weight. I already knew that the Lake was overloaded carrying me, Dave and his ever-present, donut-sucking dog. Takeoffs on land were exciting enough. On water I was worried the airplane would either not float or, at best, become a permanent boat.

Dave was carrying a duffel when we met on the ramp.

"What's in the bag?" I asked.

"Lunch," he replied.

"We can't take it," I said firmly. I had already spent part of the morning removing the rear seat from the airplane to reduce the weight but I had added paddles, an anchor and rope.

"And can we leave the hound here for this one?" I asked hopefully.

"No, but if we can't take off from the lake, you can leave us there and fly home yourself," he said, "if we can take the lunch."

"How would you get home?"

"My wife will be going up on the weekend."

Dave opened the bag. "Sandwich?" he offered, holding out a foot-long meatball sub. He was grinning. "If we eat a couple now, the bag will weigh less."

"No!" I exclaimed. "I just had breakfast."

Dave threw the bag in the back of the Lake. He and Whiskey waddled toward the office while I fueled his airplane. We had already calculated that the cottage was an hour and a half away. We would be gone about four hours. I filled the tanks so we would have enough gas for the round trip and some practising in between. Then I joined Dave in the office. He was dropping one-liners on Leanne.

"Ever wonder how seedless grapes reproduce?"

"No," she replied.

"Me either," he said with a laugh, "but tell me if you find out."

"Okay Ace," I said, "here's the plan. Your genius insurance agent will only count hours between takeoffs and landings on water as seaplane flying."

"Okay, point me north, I'm ready."

"Well, the summer isn't long enough for you to accumulate 10 hours, 30 minutes at a time so we're going to perform Circus's first waterdrome departure."

"The only water here is Lake Ontario and you said it was too rough most of the time."

"It's too rough today but the Circus Airport Waterdrome is calm."

"I don't know what you're talking about."

The nose came up and the Lake hauled itself out of the pond.

"You will. Let's go."

I signed us out and told Leanne that we'd be back by two o'clock.

Dave hoisted Whiskey into the back of the Lake. He curled up with his head on the duffel. Dave started the engine and turned on the radio to call for taxi instructions.

"Ask for one circuit before a northbound departure on a VFR crosscountry."

Barry was working in the tower. He gave us Runway 24. The takeoff run used the usual 4,000 feet. I selected the landing gear "up" as we approached the perimeter fence. The tree line was next.

"Turn left for the corner of the field," I yelled through the intercom.

"I'm turning, I'm turning."

The overloaded Lake's vertical speed was a few inches per minute.

"Do you want a touch and go?" Dave asked.

"Splash and go," I replied. "See the pond beside Runway 24?" I asked, pointing out Dave's side window as we turned downwind.

185

"I'd call it a bird bath," Dave replied squinting at the man-made pond.

"Well it's 800 feet long and two hundred feet wide," I shouted, "and we're going to do a touch and go on the hull with the wheels up."

"From here it looks like 80 feet by 10 feet."

"I measured it."

"I thought I was crazy," he said, shaking his head. He looked at the pond again and then at me. "You have control," he said lifting his hands and feet off the controls. "I'm not doing it."

I flew the airplane and called the tower.

"Delta Uniform Delta downwind for a touch and go in the pond next to Runway 24."

"You're crazy," Barry replied from the control tower.

"It's an insurance requirement," I answered calmly.

"Any manoeuvring other than on the active runway is at your discretion Uniform Delta. You're cleared for a low and over parallel to Runway 24, wind 230 at 15."

"Uniform Delta."

I planned to carry extra speed and just touch the nose on the surface for a second. I figured that at 100 mph I had about five seconds to clear the manmade bank surrounding the pond, dip the hull and clear the bank on the other side. I left the gear and the flaps up and kept the power on. As we approached on final, the Lake was accelerating. The pond was looking smaller. It was coming up fast. I almost chickened out but I decided that we had nothing to lose. If I missed the surface, we could find water somewhere along the way.

We crossed the nearside levie, I applied full power and pushed forward on the control wheel. The Lake obliged a little better than I had anticipated. Instead of kissing the surface, the hull whacked the pond. Water splashed up from both sides. The airplane slowed considerably. I pulled back. The nose came up and the Lake hauled itself out of the pond.

"Yahoo!" Dave shouted. "Can I try it?"

"No!" I yelled back.

Chapter Twenty-nine

THE SUBMARINE

After our splash and go in the Circus Airport sewage lagoon, Dave took control and spent the next ten minutes climbing the Lake to 2,000 feet. We flew around the end of Lake Ontario, more to avoid the air traffic at Toronto than the rough water in the great lake. At Derry, we headed north.

Dave looked down at the cars on the highway below. He had bought the Lake to wing his way over the traffic to his cottage. It was also the reason he had paid so much to have it refurbished. The fact that we were going barely faster than cars could not suppress his enthusiasm. We were flying to his cottage. We were living his dream.

"This is great!" he yelled over the intercom. "It sure beats being stuck in traffic!" When he tired of watching the cars, he switched to jokes. "My mother-in-law is the only one I know who looks worse than her passport photo," he said with a laugh.

"I didn't know that," I replied to humor him.

"Oh yah, her facial features don't know the value of teamwork."

Too many jokes later, we arrived over Dave's cottage. The area was typical of the country north of Toronto. Dotted with numerous odd-shaped lakes, the rocky bush was unsuitable for agriculture but was picturesque vacation land. Dave's cottage was one of several tucked around his lake. I had agreed to fly there because Dave had promised that the lake was over two miles long and had low shorelines. He was right. I could tell from the ripples on the water that we had the added bonus of a fresh breeze blowing down the middle. It was a weekday so there was no boat traffic on the water. It was a floatplane paradise.

I had Dave set up a low approach to the lake. We flew the length of it just above the surface checking for rocks and deadheads. Dave did an overshoot and circled around for a landing. During the pre-landing check, he made sure the wheels were retracted, extended the flaps and added power to make a shallow, nose-up approach.

Water splashed over the cabin, obliterating all view.

In our pre-flight briefing, I had warned Dave to pull back just as the flying boat's hull touched the surface, otherwise there was the danger of the airplane digging a hole in the water and following it to the bottom like it almost did in the sewage pond. I also warned him that if he pulled back too hard, he'd set up a porpoising action that would make the airplane hop, skip and jump like a bucking horse.

As Dave skimmed the Lake over the surface, I was poised on the controls to correct his over-corrections. The hull touched the water. The airplane dug in. Dave pulled back. We were thrown against our seat belts. I could feel the overweight bloodhound bump into the back of my seat. Water splashed over the cabin, obliterating all view. I pulled on my control wheel but Dave already had the elevator against the stop.

The water drained off the windows to reveal that we were stopped on the surface. The overloaded Lake had not plunged to the bottom or skipped back into the air. It had buried itself in the water and plowed to a dead stop.

Most of my seaplane experience had been in airplanes that sat high on floats. I was surprised to be looking at the shallow waves lapping at the side of the hull just below my elbow. It was like being in a half-submerged submarine.

"Hey, that was great!" Dave enthused. "Why don't we taxi over to the cottage?" he asked, dropping the water rudder. "There's some beer and sausage in the fridge."

I could see water was leaking in the bottom of my door. I looked at Dave's side. "What's that wet stuff under your door?" I asked.

"Hey, a little water," he laughed. "I guess we're on a lake."

"Well let's skip the beer and sausage and try a takeoff. Forward motion will keep us from sinking. Add power now and we'll taxi downwind."

The water line should have been well below the doorsills. Dave moved the throttle lever ahead. The thrust from the overhead propeller pushed the nose deeper into the water. Waves broke over the bow.

"Pull the control wheel back," I said loudly.

It didn't make any difference. The breeze from behind us was cancelling the effect of the prop blast over the elevator. I called for more power. Dave gave me a questioning look. "If we get enough thrust and motion happening, you'll be able to lever the nose up with the elevator," I said.

"If the airplane doesn't sink first," he replied.

"We're sinking anyway," I said.

Dave added more power. The water over the bow washed halfway to the windshield before the nose finally lifted. Dave was at half throttle. "Give it more!" I yelled over the noise. "Now we know it won't deep six on us."

Dave pushed the throttle further. The Lake plowed along noisily. The door leaks stopped. "Try some shallow turns for practice," I suggested.

Dave squeezed the rudder pedals, gingerly at first and then with more gusto. The Lake wallowed back and forth. Being so low in the water, it was slow to respond but stable.

"Try a 360 to the left," I barked, "but when you turn into the wind, drop the right aileron to lift the outside float."

Dave executed several turns. He found that he couldn't hurt the airplane. When he turned too tight, the wingtip float on the outside of the turn would bury itself in the water counteracting Dave's rud-

189

der inputs. We did circles and figure eights to the end of the lake.

"When you're ready for the takeoff, don't slow down," I yelled. "Just turn around and go."

During our pre-flight briefing at The Flying Circus, I had told Dave that he would have to be super smooth on the controls. "Minimize the control movements and you'll minimized the drag," I had said.

I knew some cowboy bush pilots believed they could force over-loaded floatplanes onto the step by madly moving the elevator control like an epileptic puppeteer. But that was in floatplanes and this was an under-powered, overloaded flying boat.

"My mother-in-law is so ugly, her face is her chaperone."

"Just fly the airplane," I replied.

"Her stomach went for its own career."

With that, Dave turned the airplane into the wind, raised the water rudder and hit full power. The noise level increased, the speed did not. Dave applied enough right rudder to keep the airplane pointed straight down the lake. He held the nose up and waited. We both waited.

"Try different nose up attitudes to see if you can find one that'll give us some acceleration," I offered, "but keep the control movements to a minimum."

Dave lowered the nose slightly. We could both feel the airplane slow down as the bow dug in. He raised the nose, the deceleration stopped. He pulled the control wheel back further. The tail touched the water and the airplane slowed down. He eventually found that the original attitude maintained our speed. We waited some more. The Lake plowed beyond the halfway point. There was no evidence of the hull climbing onto the step. Dave looked at me. I checked the instrument panel. The engine gauges indicated we were getting full power.

"Try different rudder positions," I barked.

Dave pushed the left rudder pedal. The right float dug in and the airplane slowed down. He pushed the right rudder pedal. The left float dug in and we slowed down some more. By now we were running out of lake.

"Cut the power and we'll turn around," I yelled.

Dave pulled the throttle back, the nose dug in, water shot over the cabin and we stopped. Water started leaking in under the doors.

"We could spend the afternoon with the beer and sausage in the

THE SUBMARINE

cottage until the cooler air comes this evening," Dave offered hopefully.

"No," I replied, "turn us around and give me a high-speed taxi to the other end of the lake.

"Okay," he shrugged.

We plowed back to the downwind end. "I haven't spoken to my mother-in-law for a year," Dave said. "I didn't want to interrupt her," he laughed.

"I have control!" I barked.

"You've got it!" Dave shouted back.

I applied full power, eased the airplane to the right side of the lake and then turned left. Once we were running straight into the wind, the airplane settled into a steady plow. We were obviously not going to get airborne. I pushed the control wheel forward. The nose went down and the airplane slowed. A bow wave built up in front. I pulled back. The nose climbed the bow wave. The airplane accelerated slightly. When the nose started to sink, I pushed forward, built up another bow wave and pulled back. We slowed and accelerated a little more. I timed consecutive pitching movements to match the bow wave. This set up a porpoising action that helped build up speed and lift the hull further and further out of the water.

"Wahoo!" Dave whooped as I rocked the nose up and down.

By the time we were halfway down the lake, I had managed to lever the airplane onto the step and had the hull planing on the surface.

"That's the spirit!" Dave yelled excitedly. "Let 'er rip!"

I neutralized the controls to minimize the drag. The airplane stopped accelerating. I adjusted the pitch attitude up and down. The lake slowed down both times. I had heard of cowboy bush pilots yawing on the step to lift one wing up at a time in an overloaded airplane. I applied left rudder. The Lake started curving toward the shoreline. The right wingtip float lifted clear of the water. We accelerated slightly. We were three quarters of the way down the lake and headed toward Dave's cottage on the left side. I yawed right. The left float lifted clear. I straightened the airplane out. We were gaining speed slowly with just the middle of the hull still in the water. The end of the lake was approaching fast as we lifted off. I aimed for the lowest trees on the shoreline. The Lake inched its way over them with a few feet to spare.

191

I aimed for the lowest trees on the shoreline.

"All right!" Dave yelled. "Let's land again and celebrate with lunch at the cottage."

"Not until we see if you can get it to take off. You have control. Do a circuit for a landing."

"Okay, but if I can't it's because I'm too weak from a lack of food."

Dave flew a circuit and set up for a landing. When the hull touched the surface, water shot over the cabin and we were thrown against our seat belts. Whiskey slammed into our seat backs as the airplane plowed into the lake to a quick stop. Dave extended the water rudder and turned us around. He pulled out a submarine sandwich that he had hidden in his jacket pocket.

"Snack?" he asked holding it out to me.

There was water leaking under my door. "You eat while I taxi us back," I said.

"I've got another one in my other pocket," he replied.

"Save it in case we can't get out of here," I said. I retracted the water rudder and applied power. "I'll give you from here to the end of the lake," I yelled. "Then I want you to take control."

192

It was no contest for the sandwich. It was gone in three big bites. Dave wiped his hands on his pants and then reached for the controls. His mouth was stuffed full so he nodded to me that he was taking over.

"Ease over to the right," I yelled, "and then do a left one eighty turn into the takeoff."

He nodded that he understood. He pushed the rudder pedals. The Lake turned right and then obediently plowed around into the wind. With full power on, Dave started rocking the elevator control in and out. It took him a while to match the inputs to the pitching motion of the bow. By the time we reached the halfway point, he had the idea. By the three-quarter mark, he had the Lake on the step but we were running out of room. He glanced in my direction. I drew my hand across my throat in a scything motion. He cut the power.

"Boy, that sure is hard work," he sighed. "Do you want to stop at the cottage for a beer?"

"No," I said. "If you get us airborne on the next try, we'll have enough time and fuel to make it back to The Flying Circus. I have students booked this afternoon."

"Do you think we'll get out all right?" he asked.

"Yes, but you'll have to stop jawing and add power. There's water leaking under my door."

"You take it," he said lifting his hands from the control wheel. He pulled out the other sandwich from his jacket. "If we're not staying, I might as well eat this. Do you want half?"

"No thank you."

I taxied the Lake while Dave ate. He took control, turned us around at the end and by pitching and yawing the flying boat just right, got us airborne and over the trees. We flew home. When we were approaching the Circus Control Zone, I told Dave to ask for a low and over beside the runway.

"Low and over Runway 24 approved Delta Uniform Delta," Barry replied from the tower. Then he added, "Splash and go in the lagoon at the pilot's discretion."

"Can I do this one?" Dave asked.

"Sure," I replied, "but go in with lots of power and speed and just touch the surface. Don't let it dig in."

"We're lighter now," Dave chuckled. "I ate those sandwiches."

Our water work at the cottage had cleaned off most of the lagoon goo from our departure dip in the sewage pond. Dave loaded it up again. He flew a splash and go. The Lake dug in, we both pulled back. The airplane hopped back out of the pond streaming brown water and wet toilet paper. We did a circuit and landing. When we stepped out of the airplane, the smell told us why the fuselage had turned from white to beige. Later that day, I turned the hose on the airplane. The bum wad came off but the brown stuff remained.

Dave and I repeated the trip to his cottage twice, splashing through the Circus Airport sewage lagoon at the beginning and ending of each flight. We flew one of the lessons in the evening to experience the effect of glassy water. On that lesson, the Lake wouldn't come unstuck from the surface until we had roared up and down enough to make our own rough water. By the end of the month, we had finished the required flight time, Dave was proficient at water handling and the Lake's fuselage, tail and wing roots were permanently brown.

"It looks like tooth decay," Dave complained.

"It's good advertising," I replied.

Chapter Thirty

CAN'T TAKE A JOKE?

"Circus Ground, this is Foxtrot Tango Victor Hotel on The Flying Circus ramp, request taxi instructions for a Special VFR Flight in the circuit."

"Tango Victor Hotel, Circus Ground, are you familiar with Notice to Airmen 26/78? The Circus Control Zone will be closed in 28 minutes."

"Affirmative," the student pilot replied. On the office radio monitor we could hear Barry McDay coaching him in the background. "We'll do circuits until the airport is closed."

"Tango Victor Hotel, roger, Runway 28 for you. The latest weather on the hour is ceiling 500 broken, visibility 15 plus, wind 300 degrees at 15 gusting to 20, altimeter 30.14. Your Special VFR clearance is on request. Taxi via Charlie, Bravo to hold short of Runway 24. Call the tower for clearance across."

"Tango Victor Hotel," the student replied, "will hold short of Runway 24."

Barry and the student taxied out, were given clearance to cross Runway 24 and Special VFR Clearance to take off on Runway 28 for circuits. They departed and circled close to the airport at 400 feet above ground, staying just below the broken layer of clouds. They were in sight of the airport during each circuit. This gave the dignitaries assembled on the ramp in front of Circus's little terminal building something to watch.

The gathering on the ground was waiting to greet Britain's Queen Mother. She was scheduled to arrive in a military VIP aircraft from Toronto. During a half-day stay, she was to visit the local government experimental farm and officially open the refurbished town armory. For Circus it was a big event. The citizens living along the planned motorcade route from the airport had spruced up their gardens and cleaned up their junk. Some had even painted their houses for the occasion. The Circus council had voted to spend town money on beautifying the public property that she would pass. The Circus Airport had been included in the funding. Airport Manager Barney Swallow had bought shrubs and flowers and hired his teenage relatives to plant them with the town money. The Circus Chronicle had been running a special daily countdown section about the planned visit over the past month.

The government had issued a Class Two Notice to Airmen showing that the airspace along the flight path planned for the Queen Mother's aircraft from Toronto and around the Circus Airport would be closed when she was in the air.

As the big day approached, preparations had intensified. Barney's family work crew trimmed the airport grass to an inch of its life. The RCMP visited to make security arrangements. Barney was told that he would be allowed to stand in the group of local dignitaries officially greeting the Queen Mother as she deplaned. He bought his first new suit since the end of World War II. It was announced that the Circus schools would be closed so children could line the Queen Mother's route to the armory.

The big day dawned cloudy and cool. A cold front had gone through the night before, leaving clear visibility under a low-lying layer of fluffy broken cloud. It was business as usual at The Flying Circus. Since the airspace around the airport would be closed for only a few minutes during the arrival and departure of the VIP airplane, we had booked a regular slate of flying lessons. The low cloud caused some cancellations but Barry McDay planned to fly a circuit lesson with a student around the time of the Queen Mother's arrival. The newly-endorsed flying instructor was keen. Although the regulation minimum ceiling of cloud was 1,000 feet for visual flying in a control zone, he knew that the tower could grant permission for Special VFR flying with the cloud as low as 500 feet as long as there was no instrument traffic arriving or departing.

During their third circuit, the controller cleared them for a full stop landing. "The airport will be closed in four minutes, Tango Victor Hotel. You're cleared to land on Runway 28."

"Tango Victor Hotel."

"Circus Tower," a new, deeper voice said on the frequency. "This is Canadian Forces Four, over."

"Can Force Four, Circus, go ahead."

"Canadian Forces Four is a Cosmopolitan 14 miles north of the Circus Beacon. We have a royal on board and have been cleared for the NDB Approach Runway 06."

196

"Can Force Four, roger, we check you are the royal flight. The Circus weather, a special at 15:20 Zulu, 500 broken, 15 plus, altimeter 30.14, wind 300 degrees at 15 gusting to 20, clouds cumulus eight. I have a Special VFR Cherokee doing a full stop on Runway 28. The aircraft is on final now and should not be a factor. Call by the Circus Beacon outbound."

"We'll call beacon outbound," the deep voice acknowledged, "Canadian Forces Four."

The Cosmopolitan was the Canadian version of the Consolidated Convair, a large twin-engine turboprop. The pilots were probably the most experienced in the air force VIP squadron. The voice on the frequency was understated to the point of sounding condescending.

The NDB instrument approach to Runway 06 was the only one available at Circus. It was a non-precision approach utilizing a transmitter four miles away on the other side of the city off the end of Runway 06. Because of the obstructions in the city, the minimum altitude on the final approach was 579 feet above the ground.

Barry and his student landed and were given taxi instructions to the Flying Circus ramp. "If it's okay with you," the student said with coaching from the background, "we'd like to pull off to the side, shut the engine down and monitor the radio so we can go back up again after the VIP transport has landed."

"Okay," the controller said, "shut down where you are and remain well clear of Runway 06"

"Tango Victor Hotel."

"Canadian Forces Four is by the Circus Beacon outbound," the deep voice announced.

"Can Force Four, roger, call by the beacon inbound."

"Canadian Forces Four," the pilot replied and then added in an unyielding tone. "The airport should be closed to other traffic by NOTAM. Our security people would like the Cherokee clear of all runways and taxiways."

There was silence for a moment. Barry was too sharp to take that one lying down. He took the microphone from his student. "NOTAM 26/78 closes the airspace around the airport during your arrival," he declared calmly. "The airport is open to ground traffic; otherwise nobody would be able to drive in to pick up your passenger."

More silence.

197

"Tango Victor Hotel requests taxi clearance to the Circus ramp," Barry said.

"Thank you Tango Victor Hotel," the controller said. "You are cleared to the Circus ramp."

"Tango Victor Hotel."

The Cherokee taxied onto our ramp, turned around and shut down. The Cosmos flew a procedure turn above the cloud to line up with Runway 06.

"Canadian Forces Four by the Circus Beacon inbound."

"Can Force Four, you are cleared to land Runway 06, winds 300 at 10 to 15, check gear down. Circling for Runway 24 is available."

"Canadian Forces Four, gear down."

With the tail wind, the Cosmos had a ground speed of 140 knots, more than two miles a minute. The pilot had less than two minutes to find the airport. If he saw it when it was too late to land on 06, he could circle to land in the other direction.

The approach was doomed to failure. Despite the good weather under the clouds, the Cosmopolitan pilot was not allowed to descend below 579 feet on his final approach until he had visual contact with a runway. If he did not have a clear view of the airport, he was obliged by air regulations to execute an overshoot.

The big airplane lumbered though the broken layer of clouds. The pilots probably caught the occasional glimpse of the ground but with the Queen Mother on board, it would not be enough to justify ducking below the obstruction clearance altitude. In the office, we could hear the deep-throated turboprop engines passing overhead. The dignitaries waiting on the ramp would be hearing them too.

"Canadian Forces Four is on the missed approach."

"Can Force Four, roger, contact Toronto Centre on 133.3

"Canadian Forces Four."

The pilot's voice remained flat calm but you could imagine the fast and furious communications on the other radios in the aircraft. By the time the Cosmos flew back to Toronto and the Queen Mother was driven to Circus, her half-day would be nearly over.

Barry's student came on the frequency. The Cherokee was still shut down on our ramp. "Tango Victor Hotel requests Special VFR for circuits."

"Tango Victor Hotel, standby," the controller replied.

A minute later the voice-from-the-boots came back on the fre-

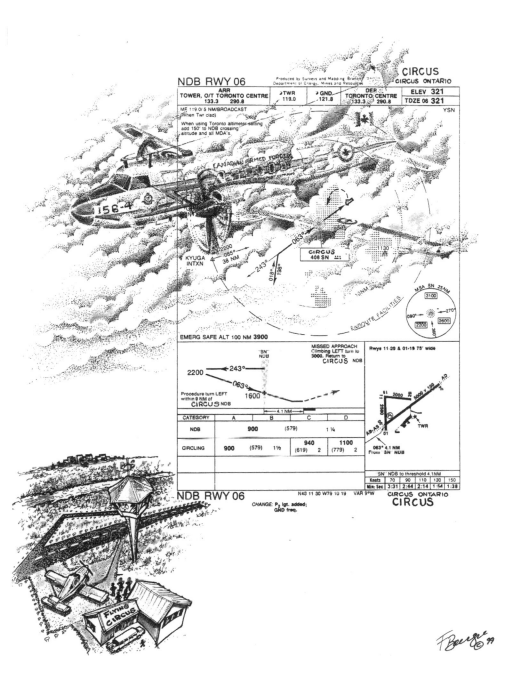

quency. "Circus Tower, this is Canadian Forces Four. We have been cleared to the Circus Airport for the NDB approach to Runway 06."

The voice was still deep and calm but not as deep and not as calm as it had been. He was coming back for another try, spurred on perhaps by the fleeting glimpses of the ground during his low and over of the airport or maybe by the embarrassment of not being able to land at an airport where a student pilot was flying circuits.

"Can Force Four, roger, call by the Circus Beacon outbound."

"Canadian Forces Four. Tell the weatherman to give us another special weather observation."

"He's already out there, Can Force Four. We'll pass it on as soon as we get it."

"Canadian Forces Four."

"Tango Victor Hotel, Special VFR is not available due to inbound IFR traffic. Say your intentions."

"Tango Victor Hotel." This time it was Barry talking. "We'll wait until the traffic has completed another missed approach."

The controller ignored the barb. "Roger," was all he said.

"Canadian Forces Four is by the Circus Beacon outbound."

"Can Force Four, roger, the Circus weather, a Special at 15:32 is 500 broken, 15 plus, wind 300 at 15 gusting to 20, altimeter 30.15, clouds cumulus eight. Call by the Circus Beacon inbound."

"Canadian Forces Four."

Four minutes of dead air time followed while the Cosmos pilot flew a procedure turn to line the aircraft up with Runway 06.

"Canadian Forces Four, by the beacon inbound."

"Can Force Four, roger, you are cleared to land Runway 06, check the gear is down."

"Gear down, Canadian Forces Four."

The weather hadn't changed and the minimum altitude rules hadn't changed so there was no reason for the pilot to make the landing. The Cosmos flew over the airport in the cloud and executed a missed approach.

"Canadian Forces Four is on the overshoot."

"Can Force Four, roger, are you heading back to Toronto this time?"

"Affirmative," was the clipped reply.

"Call Toronto Centre 133.3."

"Canadian Forces Four."

There was no silence before Barry had his student back on the frequency. "Circus Tower, Tango Victor Hotel requests Special VFR for circuits."

"Circus tower, Canadian Forces Four," the deep voice cut in. The pilot sounded annoyed that this pesky student in the Cherokee wanted to depart on a training flight when he couldn't land an IFR approach.

"Victor Hotel, standby. Can Force Four go ahead."

"Is your weather improving at all? Are the clouds breaking up?"

"From here it doesn't look like it, Can Force Four. Do you want me to send the weatherman out for another observation?"

"Negative, we don't have time."

"Can Force Four, this is Tango Victor Hotel." It was Barry McDay's voice. "Do you want us to fly over to Toronto and pick the old girl up for you? We've got room in the back seat."

There was no reply. "I guess that was a 'No,' Barry," the tower controller said.

"I guess he can't take a joke," Barry replied.

Chapter Thirty-one

WHALE HARPOONED

Cheers went up from half the group.

The end of the month brought the official weigh-off at the end of the diet contest that I had cooked up with Dave Michelin. We held it before he departed on his first solo flight to his cottage. We had advertised the competition in The Flying Circus newsletter just for fun. The article generated interest with the staff and customers. Side bets had developed. Half the group wagered on the fact that Dave ate too many donuts and the other half bet that he had more to lose.

There were several people present for the weigh-off. Dave wouldn't allow anyone to see the numbers except Leanne. He made me go first. I climbed on the scales behind the counter. Leanne raised an eyebrow in surprise. She wrote down what she saw. Dave made me go back to the other side of the counter. He climbed on. Leanne's eyes popped.

"You win," she said to me.

Cheers went up from half the group. "How much did I lose?" I asked.

"You didn't," she said. "You win because you only gained four pounds."

"Well, Dave," I said, "I'd offer you double or nothing but if you gain any more, the Lake won't fly."

"I didn't know donut holes had so many calories," Dave said. "I'm going back to cream filled."

The next week Dave flew to his cottage with Whiskey. Several days later he returned to The Flying Circus with a sheepish grin, a box of donuts and no airplane. He told us what had happened.

He had flown north and splashed down on the lake without any trouble. "The Tooth Ferry flies better without a heavy-duty instructor," he declared. "The doors didn't even leak but we should have practised more docking. I approached the cottage with the shoreline on my left, just like you showed me but I had brain fade. I thought I was driving my boat. I charged the dock and reached for the power lever to throw it in reverse," he said with a chuckle.

There was no reverse. The two ton flying boat continued unabated. The bow slammed into the floating wooden wharf and pushed it down. The airplane climbed over it and dropped into the lake on the other side. The damage would have been restricted to paint off the keel except for the saggy old diving board at the end of the dock. The pontoon hanging under the right wing caught the diving board and was sliced in half. When the airplane came to rest on the other side of the dock, Dave's weight kept the right wing out of the water. He paddled the Lake back to the dock and tied up.

Dave and Whiskey holed up in the cottage until his wife went up on the weekend.

The pontoon under the right wing was sliced in half by the diving board.

"That's four days without a donut. I thought old Whiskey was going to pass out. I kept him alive with sausage, popcorn and beer but it's not the same."

When Dave got back to Circus he called Darcy. The aircraft mechanic drove up north with tools, a helper and another pontoon. They spent two days eating and sleeping at the cottage while replacing the float. I was in The Flying Circus office when Darcy flew in with the repaired Lake. Dave was there to meet him. The new float was painted in green chromate primer.

"It looks like a rotten tooth hanging below the wing," I said.

"Hey, it looks better than the last time I saw it," Dave replied.

Darcy shut the engine down and jumped out of the cockpit. "She's all fixed up for you Dave. I'll paint the float to match the airplane when the cottage season is over."

"Great, thank you," Dave said.

"He just wants to see if you'll whack the diving board again before he paints it," I said with a laugh.

"It won't happen," Darcy said.

"You figure he's learned his lesson?"

"No, he's a pilot, same as you. I took the diving board off the dock."

204

Chapter Thirty-two

CHAINSAW CHARLIE

The biographies of famous pilots often describe how they rode their bicycles to the local airport to be around airplanes as dirt-poor kids. They'd haul gas cans in their bare feet and wash airplanes all day for the chance of a 10-minute flight.

Henry and I believed when we started a flying school, that aviation-crazed youngsters would bicycle to the Circus Airport looking to pump our gas and wash our airplanes. They didn't come. Somewhere on the way to the twenty-first century, youngsters found something else to do. So we washed and fueled the airplanes ourselves. Then Barry did it while working on his Instructor Rating. Then he got too busy flying. After that we wiped off the occasional windshield but let the grime build up on the airframes.

On a bad weather day, Henry and I were cleaning windshields in the hangar. It was how we held business meetings, talking more than rubbing. A stocky teenager walked through the hangar pedestrian door. He was dressed and built like a young lumberjack. His shiny black hair looked like it had been combed for a special occasion. I immediately sized him up as not having enough money to afford flying lessons. He stopped inside, squared his unlaced boots to us and announced, "The lady in the office said I'd find you in here."

"What can we do for you?" Henry asked cheerfully.

The youngster surveyed the overlapping high wing/low wing aircraft parked in the hangar. "You need me to wash these airplanes," he declared with a loud nervousness. "They're dirty, eh?"

"Well you're right about the dirt," Henry replied with a smile. He put down his cleaning cloth and walked toward the teenager. "I'm Henry Rains," he said, sticking out his hand.

The boy took it in a bent-arm grip that made Henry wince. "Charlie Papineau."

"Pleased to meet you Charlie," Henry said, nursing his hand. "This is my partner," he added indicating in my direction.

"Hi, Charlie," I said waving from the other side of the airplane I

205

was cleaning. I stayed there rather than risk my fingers. Charlie gave me a nod and looked at the floor.

"What do you know about airplanes?" Henry asked.

Charlie looked up but avoided eye contact with Henry. "Lots. I own two of 'em, eh?"

"You own two airplanes?" Henry answered in surprise.

"Yup. I'm buildin' 'em." Then his voice dropped a little, "Well, the first one didn't turn out too good. Designed 'er a few years back myself from plywood but she's too heavy, eh? So I sent for plans outta Mechanics Digest, the Fly Baby. She's goin' to be a beauty."

"Tell me Charlie, how old are you?"

I knew why Henry had asked. This son-of-Paul Bunyan looked anywhere from 17 to 27 years old.

"Thirteen," Charlie replied, "but I'll be fourteen this fall."

"Are you still in school?"

"Not right now, sir. It's summer holidays, eh."

Henry smiled at the reply. "Are you going back to school in September?"

"Yes, sir. I'm goin' to finish my Grade Eight," Charlie said, blushing a little. "I'll do better this time."

"Well Charlie Papineau, we'll give you a try at washing our dirty airplanes. When can you start?"

Charlie shoved up both sleeves on his checkered shirt. "Where's the hose?"

"In the corner," Henry replied and pointed. "The bucket, soap and brush are with it. Do this one first," he added, indicating Cherokee Tango Victor Hotel.

Henry helped Charlie get started while I continued to clean windows.

"How much time do you have today, Charlie?" Henry asked.

"Until supper."

"How often are you available?"

"Most days, when I'm not helping mom around the house."

During this short conversation, Charlie had filled the bucket with soap and water and began to attack TVH. He scrubbed with the soapy brush in one hand and rinsed with the hose in the other. The airplane rocked while he worked.

"Do a good job today," Henry said, "and you're hired. Be careful that you don't break off any antennas and don't use the brush on the windows, they're plastic."

206

The airplane rocked while he worked.

"Yes sir," Charlie replied without stopping, "I know."

Henry and I continued to clean windows while Charlie scrubbed. We found out that he was the second oldest of eight kids in a family from the Canadian east coast. He told us the problem with his first airplane was that the plywood was too thick and his chainsaw was too dull. "She's a bit rough, eh," he said.

By the time we had finished the windshields, Charlie was on his second airplane. He worked quickly and was doing a good job. We left him on his own with instructions to wash the three flying school aircraft. We went back to the office where Dave Michelin was holding court with Leanne, a box of donuts and Whiskey.

"Do you know how many successful flights have to be made to obtain a pilot licence?" he was asking Leanne when we walked in.

"No," she answered.

"All of them," he said and then roared at his own joke.

"Hi Dave," I said, "are you ready for a ground briefing?"

207

Dave had booked his first lesson for a Night Endorsement Course. "Sure, but let me get this straight," he said. "I want to learn to fly at night so you start me with instrument flying during day-light with a hood over my eyes so I can't see outside but we can't fly today because the weather is bad and we can't see outside?"

"Correct. Did you study that material on the flight instruments?"

"Do Siamese twins use extra body shampoo?" he asked.

I ignored his question and said, "That's why I had you come any-way. We can do a ground briefing on the material you didn't study."

I taught Dave while Henry did some paperwork. A while later he went to the hangar to check on Charlie. He came back shortly and caught my eye.

"When you two are done, come out to the hangar."

I had been describing the theory of the gimbaled gyro in the atti-tude indicator. Dave's eyes were glazing over. "We're done now," I said.

"For sure," Dave said, waking up and looking in the empty box, "we're out of donuts."

Dave, Whiskey and I followed Henry to the hangar. Inside Charlie had finished washing the flying school aircraft and was attacking Dave's Lake. He had finished one side of the brown-streaked white fuselage. The transformation was amazing. The clean side gleamed.

"Wow," Dave exclaimed. He looked at Charlie who had stripped down to T-shirt and jeans. "Where did this guy come from?"

"Charlie, this is Dave Michelin," Henry said.

Charlie straightened up for a moment and gave Dave a nod. "Pleased to meet you, sir."

"Look at the bottom," Henry said pointing under the Lake.

I bent down and looked forward from the tail. The former brown hull was clean and bright.

"That's unbelievable!"

Charlie smiled at the compliment. "Oven cleaner," he volun-teered. "That brown stuff was crusted on worse than a toilet at a green apple growers' convention. The oven cleaner took 'er off. I had some with me."

"You're doing a great job, Charlie" I said.

"Yah," Dave agreed. "It sure needed it."

"I'd like to wax 'er when I'm done," Charlie said. "It puts on a protective coating."

"We'll get him some wax," Henry said to Dave.

"I'll wax 'er tomorrow when the weather is dryer," Charlie offered.

"That's great, Charlie," Dave said, "thank you."

"You're welcome, sir."

Dave turned to me. "I like that. How come you don't call me 'Sir'?"

"Because you wouldn't know who I was talking to."

"You're right."

Dave, the dog and I headed back to the office. Henry stayed in the hangar with Charlie. Later he told me about their conversation when they were finishing up.

"I'm glad you came today, Charlie," Henry had said. "Consider yourself hired. Tomorrow I'll show you how to run the gas pumps. When you finish waxing the Lake, you can wax the three flying school airplanes for us. On the good weather days, you'll have to grab them between flights."

"No problem, sir."

"Are you interested in exchanging your work here for flying lessons?" Henry asked.

"I'd rather have the money if you don't mind," Charlie replied.

"No that's fine. Come to the office. We'll settle up for today and then we'll throw your bicycle in the back of my car. I'll give you a ride home."

"I don't need a ride," Charlie said.

"But I insist. It's raining out."

"I don't have a bicycle, sir," Charlie admitted, blushing a little. "Since my dad died two years ago, mom lets me drive the pick-up truck as long as I'm using it for work."

Chapter Thirty-three

I SPY

An older man walked through our office door and left it open. He stopped in the middle of the room and planted his feet well apart under a short, plump body. He looked a bit dazed. "Your airplane is following me," he declared.

Henry and I exchanged puzzled looks. We could hear the Cessna 172 taxiing onto The Flying Circus ramp. Barry was returning with a student. "I don't know what you're talking about, sir," I said.

"It's spying on me," he continued. His voice was edgy but not loud. "Everywhere I go, it's there, overhead, watching."

"You must be mistaken," I replied. I didn't know what else to say.

"No, I'm not," he said. "It was over my house. I followed it here. That's the plane." He gestured out the door toward the Cessna.

I decided the man was crazy although he didn't look it. He could have passed for anyone's kindly uncle. I was about to comment on his state of mind but Henry acted first. He calmly approached him and extended his hand. "I'm Henry Rains," he said. The man accepted the handshake but didn't offer his name. "I'm the owner here," Henry said, "but I didn't know one of my airplanes was following you."

"Well it is," he replied. "When I go to the shopping plaza, it's there, watching. When I'm at the legion, it's there too. This afternoon it followed me to the post office."

"What's your name?" Henry asked.

"Andrew Penny," the man replied.

"That airplane is being used for flying lessons," Henry explained patiently. "The pilots have been practising takeoffs and landings at the airport. I don't think they were spying on anybody."

Barry walked through the open door with his student. Andrew Penny stared at them. "You were following me," he announced.

Before Barry could say anything, Henry introduced him. "Andrew, this is Barry McDay. He is one of the flying instructors here. Barry, this is Andrew Penny. We were just discussing how air-

"Your airplane is following me."

planes in the circuit are always flying over him."

"Please to meet you Mr. Penny," Barry said politely. He offered a handshake. Penny took it. "I hope we weren't disturbing you," Barry said.

"You were spying on me," Penny replied. He stuck his chin out to emphasize his statement.

Barry looked at Henry for help. "You finish with your student, Barry," Henry said. "Andrew, would you allow me to buy you a coffee? I'd like to hear more about this problem." Henry placed his hand on the man's shoulder and steered him toward the coffee maker.

"Yes, I'd like a coffee," Penny replied. "I take cream and sugar but I'll fix it myself."

Leanne was off so I went behind the desk to fill in an invoice for Barry's student. I kept one ear on the conversation at the coffeepot.

"Where do you live, Andrew?" Henry asked our visitor as he poured two cups of coffee.

"On Penny Road, north of here," the older man volunteered without hesitation. He opened a packet of sugar.

"In the old white farm house?" Henry asked.

Penny looked up from pouring sugar into his cup. "You've been spying on me too?"

"No, no, not me," Henry said quickly. He changed the subject. "You said you went to the legion. Were you in the war?"

"Yes sir," Penny said proudly. He stuck out his chest. "Queen's Rifles. Straight into Germany." He snapped his right hand in a salute.

"It must have been tough," Henry commented sincerely and sipped his coffee.

Penny switched his look from proud to suspicious. "You think I'm shell shocked. Has my wife been talking to you?"

"No, not at all," Henry said. "I'm just trying to help."

"Well you can help by telling those people to stop spying on me."

They both paused and sipped their coffee. Henry tried a different approach. "Why would they be spying on you, Andrew?"

Penny put his coffee down quickly and pointed a spirited finger at Henry. "So I'm right, they are following me!"

"I didn't say that," Henry replied quickly. "They were just flying around the airport practising takeoffs and landings."

"I saw them. They were looking at me."

"Have you ever been in a small airplane before?" Henry asked.

"No," Penny replied and picked up his coffee cup again.

"You and I should go flying. I'll show you that our airplanes are not spying on you. Would you go up with me?"

"You want me to go flying?"

"Yes."

"In one of your airplanes?"

"That's right. We can take the one that just came down."

"The one that was following me?"

"The one that was just flying around the airport."

"You want me to go right now?"

"Right now," Henry said. He took a last swig of coffee and put the cup down.

212

"Okay."

I signed out Henry and handed him the logbook and keys for the Cessna.

"Have a good flight," I said to his new passenger.

"Thank you," he replied. He sounded a bit nervous but he managed a little smile.

I watched out the office window. I could see Henry showing Penny the parts of the airplane. He helped him into the right front seat of the Cessna and then climbed into the left seat. After a few minutes the airplane's engine was started. I could hear Henry on the office monitor asking the Circus ground controller for taxi instructions for circuits. The airplane headed for the runway.

I was still in the office when they returned about 20 minutes later.

Penny was the first one through the door. He looked back at Henry and said, "So you're with the police."

"No," Henry replied loudly, "I'm not." He sounded frustrated.

"Well, you must be working for them."

"No, I'm just a pilot. I'm not working for anyone."

"You're a pilot who spies on innocent old men!" Penny declared. He approached the flight desk and looked across at me. His face was set in a scowl. "May I use your washroom?"

"Certainly," I replied, pointing to the far corner of the room. "Help yourself."

Penny shuffled toward the washroom. Henry handed me the aircraft logbook.

"I take it things didn't go well," I said.

"You got that right," he replied, shaking his head in frustration. "I thought if I stayed in the circuit, I could show him that our traffic was practising takeoffs and landings and not following him."

"I don't think it worked, Henry," I said sarcastically.

"You're not kidding. We took off from Runway 06 and turned left. I pointed to the airport and said that we would be keeping the runway in sight. He looked the other way. 'There's my house,' he said. 'I can see my backyard. I can see everything!'

"I turned downwind toward the city. 'There's the legion,' he said, 'and there's the mall, the post office and the grocery store. You have been spying on me!'

"I turned back toward the runway and landed. I don't know where he got the police idea but all I accomplished with the flight was to confirm that airplanes are following him. The poor old guy is definitely crazy but you know, from up there you can see everything. I understand his point."

"Now what are you going to do?" I asked.

"I don't think there is anything I can do. I'm just going to hope he doesn't come here every day to bother our customers or worse, start taking potshots at them."

"Well, we'll hope he's not loading the gun in the washroom right now."

Penny came out of the washroom apparently unarmed and walked over to the flight desk. He ignored Henry and looked at me with a frown.

"Did you have a nice flight?" I asked cheerfully.

The scowl softened a bit. "Yes, thank you, I did."

"Was that your first time flying?"

"Yes, it was."

"Well maybe you'll come back and fly with us again sometime."

"I'd like that," he replied pulling out a little Scotch purse. "How much do I owe you?"

Henry started to say something but I waved him off. I knew he was going give the flight away but I could see the roll of money in Penny's purse and it looked like it was all $50-dollar bills.

"A sightseeing flight for one, two or three people is $45," I said.

"That's cheap," he declared and dropped a rolled-up fifty on the counter. "No wonder there are so many airplanes up there spying."

"Would you like a receipt?" I asked, handing him a $5-dollar bill.

"No thank you," he replied. He turned and handed the five to Henry. "Thanks for the ride, sonny. I'll see you tomorrow."

"Tomorrow?"

"Yes, and I want to fly closer to my neighbor's place so I can see what he's building in his back yard."

Henry stood there with the $5-dollar bill in his hand. He didn't know what to say.

I checked the booking sheets. "Same time tomorrow would be fine," I said.

"I'll see you then," Penny said. He opened the door and walked out without closing it.

Chapter Thirty-four

THREE-RINGED CIRCUS

Barry McDay was easily bored. His instructing job at The Flying Circus kept him busy but he also worked as an air traffic controller in the local tower. The Circus Airport was not the world's busiest. There were no scheduled flights. The tower staff had to be content with handling training flights until they built enough seniority to move to a larger airport.

One morning, Henry, Ray and I were booked for lessons on the school airplanes. All three students were scheduled for take-off and landing practise at the airport. Barry was working in the control tower.

Ray and his student went first in the Cessna 172, C-LUFT. They called for taxi instructions for circuits. The wind was calm. Barry assigned them Runway 06. Henry and I followed closely behind in the two Cherokees. Barry gave us Runway 06 as well. The three aircraft taxied out and were given take-off clearances at intervals to provide adequate separation. There was no other traffic.

The Circus Airport had three runways forming a triangle: 06/24, 01/19 and 10/28. The layout was a legacy of the Commonwealth Air Training Plan from World War II. The three strips of asphalt gave the airport six runways counting each in two directions.

Barry called Henry when his Cherokee was number two behind Ray on the downwind leg for Runway 06.

"Tango Victor Hotel, Circus Tower, the winds are calm. If you'd like your own runway for circuits, you are now on a base leg for Runway 10."

There was a slight pause. "Sure," Henry's student replied. "We'll take Runway 10."

"Tango Victor Hotel, keep it in tight, you're cleared touch and go Runway 10."

"Tango Victor Hotel."

"Uniform Foxtrot Tango," Barry said to Ray's airplane, "you're number one for Runway 06, traffic ahead on the touch and go on Runway 10."

"Uniform Foxtrot Tango."

"Alpha November Delta." Barry was calling my student and me in Cherokee C-LAND. "The wind is calm, would you like your circuits on Runway 01?"

"Affirmative," I told my student to say.

"Alpha November Delta, roger, turn left now to put you on a downwind leg for Runway 01, you're number one, traffic on the touch and go Runways 10 and 06."

"Alpha November Delta."

By flying circuits on separate runways, the three aircraft crossed the other two twice during each five-minute circuit. Barry had set it up so we were spaced properly to cross paths at different times during our landing practice and at different altitudes when crossing in the air. The arrangement gave each student more landings. We didn't have to extend to follow another aircraft. It made the lessons more interesting for the instructors and the radio work kept Barry six times as busy.

"Foxtrot Tango, cleared touch and go Runway 06."

"Foxtrot Tango."

"November Delta, expect your clearance shortly for Runway 01, traffic crossing left to right on Runway 24."

"November Delta."

After a couple of circuits, my student was catching on to watching in all directions for the other traffic. Barry called us when we were climbing out from a touch and go.

"November Delta, Circus tower, the wind is calm, will you accept teardrop circuits on Runway 01/19?" Teardrop circuits involved taking off, leveling at 500 feet, turning around and landing on the same runway in the opposite direction. Barry was upping the ante on his anti-boredom exercise considerably. Teardrop circuits more than doubled the takeoff and landing practice per hour. Each airplane would be crossing the paths of the other two every two minutes. I told my student to say, "Affirmative."

"Teardrop circuits on 01/19 approved November Delta, I'll tell you when to start the turnaround."

"November Delta."

"Victor Hotel, will you accept teardrop circuits on Runway 10/28? The winds are calm."

"Victor Hotel, affirmative."

"Victor Hotel, roger, you're cleared touch and go Runway 10 for

216

Barry was upping the ante on his anti-boredom exercise considerably.

teardrop circuits on 10/28. I'll call the turnaround for Runway 28."

"Victor Hotel."

Barry gave Henry and his student the same offer for Runway 06/24. They accepted. By calling the turnarounds, Barry had some control over the separation of the three airplanes. This helped the pilots since we would have our backs to the airport half the time.

"November Delta, start your turn now, you're number one for Runway 19, traffic crossing right to left on Runways 10 and 06."

"November Delta."

"Foxtrot Tango, cleared touch and go on Runway 06. You'll see traffic left to right off Runway 10. I'll call the turn around after you take off."

"Foxtrot Tango."

And so it went. Barry kept up a continuous flow of clearances and advisories. He was doing a marvelous job of timing our turns so the student pilots could practise normal departures and approaches without worrying about the other traffic. The control tower was located on the south side of the airport and had no radar. Barry was orchestrating this web of circuits from a two-dimensional vertical view.

Ray was operating on the longest runway. He decided to test Barry's limits. "Foxtrot Tango requests a double touch and go."

"Multiple landings on Runway 24 approved Foxtrot Tango. I'll call the turn on the climbout."

"Foxtrot Tango."

Henry and I joined in. "November Delta requests stop and go on this one tower," I said.

"November Delta is cleared a full stop on Runway 01, I'll advise the go. Check traffic crossing ahead on Runway 10."

"November Delta with the traffic."

"Victor Hotel, we'd like to practise a simulated engine failure after takeoff," Henry said.

"Approved, Victor Hotel, I'll call the turnaround on your climbout."

"Victor Hotel."

"November Delta, you're cleared for takeoff Runway 01."

"November Delta."

Barry took the variations in stride. Ray turned the heat up further. When Barry called his next turnaround, he took over control of the aircraft from the student, did a steep turn and kept his speed up on the approach.

Barry saw it coming. "Foxtrot Tango, cleared full stop Runway 06. I'll advise the takeoff, traffic crossing right to left on Runway 28."

"Foxtrot Tango."

Henry pulled the same stunt on his next turnaround. I had my student extend full flaps and slow to minimum approach speed to compound the problem Henry was creating.

Barry handled it. "Foxtrot Tango, cleared for takeoff Runway 06, I'll advise the turnaround, no reply required, break, break, Victor Hotel, you're cleared full stop on Runway 10."

"Victor Hotel."

"November Delta, start your turnaround now for Runway 19."

"November Delta."

The three of us tried every combination of tight turns and slow approaches to mix Barry up. It was a clear day so we knew we could avoid each other visually. We made a game out of trying to force Barry to lose control of the situation and issue an overshoot clearance to at least one of us. Ray found the way.

218

"Victor Hotel, start your turnaround now for Runway 28."

"Foxtrot Tango," Ray answered.

"Foxtrot Tango, that was for Victor Hotel."

Ray turned anyway.

"November Delta, you're cleared touch and go Runway 19."

"Foxtrot Tango."

"Foxtrot Tango, that was not for you. Foxtrot Tango fly a 360 degree turn for spacing and re-establish yourself on final."

Ray ignored the instruction and kept coming.

"Foxtrot Tango, you're not cleared touch and go. Foxtrot Tango, pull up and go around, conflicting traffic on Runways 19 and 28."

Ray had his student start an overshoot. "Foxtrot Tango," he replied. I could hear the smile in his voice.

Barry got the last laugh. "I'll advise the turnaround for Runway 06, Foxtrot Tango," he said to Ray.

"Foxtrot Tango."

It was the end of an hour, time for all of us to do a full stop. Following Ray's missed approach and a touch and go for both Henry and I, Barry had us all flying away from the airport waiting for turnaround instructions. The tower frequency was silent. I tested the squelch on my radio. It worked. The volume was up.

"Circus tower, November Delta ready to turnaround for a full stop on Runway 01."

There was no reply.

Ray tried it. "Foxtrot Tango requests a full stop on Runway 06."

No reply.

Barry had one over on us now. We were stuck explaining to our students that our fooling around had turned their circuit lesson into a cross-country flight.

Henry pretended that he had cleared the five-mile control zone and turned around. "Circus tower, Victor Hotel is approaching the zone from the west, landing Circus."

"Victor Hotel is cleared straight in to Runway 10, the wind is calm. Call one mile final."

Ray and I tried the same thing and were given straight-in approaches to Runways 06 and 01. The timing had the three of us arriving at the airport at the same time. Barry said nothing about the conflicts. We called one mile on final within a few seconds of each other. Barry didn't reply. Now he had us pointed at each other with no clearances or instructions.

219

"Ray," I said on the frequency, "I'll overshoot high, you over-shoot low and Henry can do a climbing left turn."

The reply was a big squeal on the radio indicating two pilots were transmitting at once. I repeated my instruction and added, "Ray you reply first." He did.

"Is that all right with you, Henry?"

"Affirmative."

It was a good lesson on the importance of the control tower in a traffic conflict situation.

"Have you guys had enough?" Barry asked on the frequency.

The reply was a loud squeal on his receiver when the three of us transmitted, "Affirmative," at the same time.

Chapter Thirty-five

THE CIRCUS CHALLENGE

The Flying Circus challenged the local flying club to a water bombing contest. The bombing was Summer's idea; the challenge was Henry's. Barry thought up the scoring.

"At the university dorm they drop water-filled balloons down the stairwells on unsuspecting students," Summer said one morning out of the blue. We were sitting around waiting for bad weather to break. "It's fun. Sometimes it gets a little out of hand when you see two seniors struggling with a balloon stretched with 20 pounds of water. They often end up wearing it themselves."

"And these people are the future leaders of this country?" I asked.

"It's only water," she replied, blushing a little. "I was thinking that the ultimate drop would be from an airplane."

The fun-loving Summer was probably the "they" who dropped the balloons at the university. "So you want to fly over to the campus and drop water bombs on the students?" I asked.

"No! I was thinking that we could paint a target on the runway and try it. Anyone who wants to drop water bombs could rent an airplane. It's a good excuse to have another barbecue."

The suggestion hooked Henry into the conversation. "We could challenge the flying club," Henry said. "I'd like to lure more of their customers over here. If we run the contest and have the barbecue at The Flying Circus, their members will be forced to come here to check their scores and buy a steak."

"We could charge for the balloons and donate the money to charity," Summer added.

Henry jumped in again. "We could use the charity money to fly underprivileged children in Flying Circus airplanes."

Dave Michelin had been listening to this conversation while sitting on the couch eating donuts and drinking coffee. "I'll bring donuts," Dave offered, pulling another Bavarian cream from the box, "if there are any left." He laughed at his own comment.

The idea took off from there. Summer said that she would arrange for the church grill and ask Al Milton about steaks for the barbecue. Henry said he would talk to the flying club. We decided the "target" would be a 100-foot lime circle marked on a runway. We would sell three water-filled balloons for five dollars. Three circuits would easily fit inside a 30-minute flight. Henry suggested that contestants could enter as many times as they wanted but could only take three balloons at once. "That will increase the rental time." He was sounding more like a penny-pinching flying school owner all the time.

"Each entrant will declare whether they're on the flying club team or with the Flying Circus," Barry suggested. "The winning team would have the highest percentage of hits in the circle versus balloons bought."

"We'll get Dave to enter for the flying club," I said, jokingly.

"Sure," Dave replied with a laugh, "you can be my bombardier. The flying club will lose for sure!"

"We need some brave soul to stand out by the runway and score the hits," Summer said. No one spoke. We were all thinking of flying in the contest.

"The controllers in the tower could score it," I suggested. "They have the best view of the runway."

Barry shook his head. "It's not covered by the union contract. We'll be lucky if they let us do it at all. And don't ask me to get permission."

The group fell silent again. Chainsaw Charlie walked in from waxing airplanes in the hangar. Everyone spoke at once, "Charlie!" He stopped in his tracks. Dave heaved himself out of his seat and walked over to him holding the box of donuts. He put one arm around Charlie and waved the donuts in front of him with the other. "Charles," Dave said, "your mission, should you choose to accept it, will be to score our water bombing contest. If you should happen to be beaned in the head during the contest, this committee will disavow any knowledge of your actions. Have a donut. They will self-destruct in five seconds."

Charlie didn't know what Dave was talking about but he helped himself to a donut and stuffed it in his mouth. Summer explained to him what we had in mind. He happily agreed.

"You can even park your truck beside the runway and listen to your Stompin' Tom tapes," Henry added.

222

I was designated "permission getter". We needed the blessing of the airport manager to make a lime circle on his runway and we decided to ask the control tower supervisor if it was okay with him for a flock of airplanes to parade around his circuit dropping water-filled balloons.

I walked over to the Circus Airport Terminal to visit Barney Swallow, the airport manager. The terminal building was a small, flat-roofed structure. It looked like an oversized faded blue freight car abandoned by the railroad. Inside there were offices for the manager and his secretary, a boardroom for bimonthly Airport Commission meetings, a weather office and a customs office. The one-man weather office was equipped with leftovers retired from Canada's arctic early-warning radar line. This included Larry Livent, the weatherman. Larry had been snow-blinded years before. He predicted the weather with his bones rather than his eyes or equipment. His forecasts were usually accurate. The customs office contained an old oak desk, a chair and nothing else. It was used about once a week to clear the odd recreation or business flight into the country. The customs inspectors, alerted by the control tower staff, drove in from the international border 30 minutes away. An open foyer in the terminal held a small ticket counter for airline flights. There were no airline flights but it was there just in case.

When I walked through the terminal entrance, Gladys, the ancient airport secretary, was tap dancing across the foyer. She was swinging an umbrella and singing "The Good Ship Lollipop". When Gladys saw me, she sang louder and danced faster. If I hadn't been an airport rent payer, I might have thought it was nice that the city provided a job for a councilman's grandmother who otherwise would have been committed to an institution. I walked past her and through the open door of Barney's office.

The airport manager was sitting behind his World War II desk in his old tweed jacket and World War II regimental tie. He greeted me without getting up. I outlined our water bombing plans. "I thought we should ask permission to mark the circle on the runway," I said. I made it sound like it was a courtesy, not a necessity. Barney sat unmoving in his chair. "It's just a fun way to increase traffic at the airport," I added.

"Can't do it," he said flatly.

"Why not?" I asked politely. "The air regulations say we can if we're not creating a hazard to persons or property on the ground."

223

Barney clicked his dentures and sucked in a wheezy breath. "The air regulations dictate runway markings and they don't include a lime target circle."

"It would just be for one day and then we'll remove it," I said hopefully.

"No," he replied.

That was it. He left no opening for discussion. I stood up to leave.

"Use the lagoon," he said quietly.

I wasn't sure that I'd heard him correctly. "Use what?" I asked.

"I said you could bomb the sewage lagoon. It's bigger than 100 feet but take my word for it, most people will miss."

It was a good idea. The lagoon that Dave Michelin and I had used to start our seaplane flights was beside the main runway. It would be easy to score the splashes and there would be nothing to clean up. "That's a great idea, Barney, thanks very much. Can you join us for the contest?"

"I don't work weekends," he said without looking up. He waved me out the door.

"At least come to the barbecue," I said.

He shook his head. "Close the door on the way out before that woman drives me nuts."

I closed Barney's door and sidestepped Gladys as she tapped her way across my path to the exit doing a Betty Boop routine.

My next stop was to see Dan Stevens, the control tower chief. The Circus tower was a three-storey structure standing next to the terminal building. It looked like a two-storey cement standpipe painted white with a hexagon fish bowl on top. I walked over to the base of the tower and pushed the intercom button beside the locked door. The controller on duty asked me my business. I told him I was there to see the unit chief. He buzzed open the door lock. I walked in and started up the stairs.

I had never met Dan Stevens but I knew from talking to Barry McDay that he spent most of his time peddling his latest get-rich-quick item. His job was to manage the Circus Control Tower but union rules dictated that, as chief, Stevens was not allowed to work a microphone. All that was left to do was sit in his second-floor office with its bay window overlooking the runways and schedule the seven controllers on staff so that at least one was on duty during the two shifts a day. He had a secretary working half days to

224

"We want to run a water bombing contest against the flying club."

type up the schedule.

I reached the top of the stairs on the second floor landing. On the right, there was a metal spiral staircase to the third floor. On the left was an open door to a secretary's office. I walked into the office. A middle-aged blond in a beehive hairdo sat at a metal desk filing her nails and chewing gum. I introduced myself.

"Pleased to meet youse," she whined. "I'm Carmen."

Carmen was a throwback to the 1950s as much as Barney and Gladys were throwbacks to the 40s. She wore winged sequined glasses and a tight sweater and skirt. Her wad of chewing gum prevented her from ever closing her mouth.

"I'm here to see Dan Stevens," I said.

"Is he expecting youse?" she asked. I could see the gum clearly.

"No," I replied politely, "but if he's busy, I'll wait."

Carmen called Stevens on the intercom and told him that I was there. He said that he would be out in a minute.

"He'll be with youse in a minute," she said.

"Thank you."

I waited. Muted sounds of things being moved came from the closed door behind Carmen. After five minutes the door opened and a tall, lanky Dan Stevens stepped out.

"Welcome to Circus Tower," he said, offering me a handshake. "Come on in."

Dan Stevens was another throwback to the 1950s. His hair was brush cut; he wore a string tie, a cardigan sweater and stove-pipe pants that were pulled up too close to his armpits. I followed him into his office. The moving sounds must have come from the pile of small cardboard boxes lining the wall behind his desk.

"Have a seat," he said, gesturing to a government-issue metal chair in front of his metal desk. "I'm glad we finally get a chance to meet. I've been meaning to get over to see your new operation but I haven't had a chance."

"You're welcome anytime," I said. "The coffee is always on."

He smiled weakly and checked his finger nails. "What brings you to the tower?" he asked impatiently.

"We want to run a water bombing contest against the flying club. We were thinking of dropping water-filled balloons on the sewage lagoon. The most hits per bomb dropped wins. It's a just-for-fun excuse for our customers to fly more. We're going to have a barbecue on our ramp during the contest."

226

"Sounds like fun," Dan said. "Anything else?"

His abruptness caught me off guard. "Ah, no. We thought since it involves your controllers, that we should ask your permission to do it."

"Oh, it doesn't have anything to do with me!" he said quickly. "The controllers will handle the traffic the same way as every other day. If you want permission to hold the contest, you'll have to ask Barney Swallow, the airport manager."

"I've already talked to Barney. He said there's no problem," I lied.

"Well, there you go," Dan said. He reached back, picked up one of the boxes off the pile and placed it in front of him. "Do you need a radio?" he asked opening the box. "I can give you a really good deal on a new clock radio." He pulled out a radio encased in Styrofoam. "It's AM/FM and has a plug-in rigged to the alarm for a coffeemaker." He removed the Styrofoam and placed the radio in front of me. "They regularly retail for forty bucks but I can let you have this one for twenty-five."

It was obviously old stock. The round-faced clock and knob-tuner were mechanical instead of digital. I didn't want one. I wasn't sure if a radio purchase was part of receiving permission for the contest. Since he hadn't really given us permission, I decided to take a chance.

"We have a clock radio already," I said, "but thanks for the offer."

"How about selling them at the flying school? I can offer you a quantity for twenty bucks each."

"No thank you," I said, standing up. "If you have time, drop by during the water bombing contest and I'll buy you a steak-on-a-bun."

"I don't work weekends," he frowned.

227

Chapter Thirty-six

BOMBS AWAY

Summer McDay sent a newsletter to our customers advertising the "Bombing for Charity" contest and the barbecue. She made information posters and hung them in our office and the flying club.

The event proved to be popular. Our booking sheets filled up quickly. On the day of the contest, Henry and I went to work early to pull out and gas up the flying school airplanes. Summer arrived and set up a registration table. When Charlie came, she gave him a score sheet on a clipboard with columns for the aircraft registration, the time and the number of hits. Then she started filling balloons in the bathroom. To make them easy to handle, she only used a kilogram of water. Three fit on a paper plate although it had to be held with both hands.

Dave showed up with Whiskey and an open flat of donuts. They had already eaten five from the corner. "Did you hear about the toothless termite who walked into the bar and asked where was the bar tender?" He put the flat down. "Don't mind if I do," he said, pinching a jelly donut. He took a big bite and tossed the rest to the dog.

"Will you drop for me in this contest?" Dave asked me while chewing on the donut.

"Sure," I answered, " but it'll have to be now. I'm booked to bomb with students all day."

"Now's fine," he said. Powdered sugar flew from his mouth. "If you and Charlie pull the Tooth Ferry out, it'll give me time to wash this down with a coffee." He picked up another donut. Whiskey headed for the toilet for a drink.

"Come on Charlie, give me a hand with DUD".

Dave came out of the office balancing three balloons on a plate. "Did you hear about the plastic surgeon who hung himself?" he said to no one in particular. He handed the plate to me, "Here, as bombardier, you're in charge of these. Be careful, they cost me five dollars."

Dave flew from the left seat while I sat in the right with the plate on my lap. Whiskey rode in the back with his head on my shoulder. He was mildly interested in the balloons.

When Dave called the ground controller, he gave his registration as "Bomber One". He asked for taxi instructions for "thirty seconds over Tokyo". We took off from Runway 06. I could see the lagoon on my side of the runway with Charlie's pick-up truck parked 1,000 feet before it. He waved from beside it as we flew by. Dave did a wide, left-hand circuit to climb to 500 feet. On the downwind leg, the controller cleared us for a "low and over Runway 06." Dave turned and lined up on the lagoon along the right side of the runway.

I wasn't sure that the Lake's door could or should be opened in flight. As we approached the lagoon, I cinched up my seat belt, held the balloons with my right hand and reached over for the door handle with my left.

"Add some power, Dave," I yelled. "There'll be extra drag with the door open."

Dave obliged. I realized that I was short one hand. I needed another one to steady the plate while I threw a balloon out with one hand and held the door with the other. I picked up one balloon and balanced the others on my lap. We were approaching the lagoon.

"You'll have to call the drop," I yelled.

"Okay!"

I turned the latch without knowing if the slipstream would suck

229

the gull-wing door open or hold it closed. The door popped with a rush of wind-noise that nearly drowned out the sound of the engine behind our heads but it did not fly up. The slipstream held it closed. I pushed on it. The noise increased but the opening at the bottom of the door did not. I pushed harder; still no opening. I could feel Whiskey on my right shoulder trying to sniff the air whistling through the crack.

"Ready?" Dave shouted.

I wasn't but there was no point in answering him.

"Let 'er go!" he yelled.

I gave the door the hardest one-handed shove that I could muster. A space appeared at the bottom for a second. I thrust the balloon toward the now disappearing gap. Too late. The balloon broke against the edge of the door. Water drenched the side panel and my right leg.

I looked up. The Lake was in a turn to the left. Dave was looking down his side.

He turned to me. "Those little suckers are hard to . . ." He stopped when he spotted the water dripping down his new upholstery. "Hey, Ace," he laughed, "you're supposed to drop them outside, not inside!"

"You'll have to slow down so I can get the door open more!" I yelled. The door was still unlatched and the slipstream was howling by. The early morning air chilled my wet right leg.

"Sure! I didn't feel the drag. Slower will work," Dave replied.

He continued the left turn onto another downwind leg of the circuit. I switched hands for the next try. With my right hand on the door I could put my shoulder into it. The control tower cleared us for another pass. Dave turned toward the airport.

I picked up balloon number two in my left hand and held it ready. Dave lined up on the lagoon and slowed down to 90 mph.

"Don't wet yourself this time!" he roared.

"Just fly the airplane and call the drop," I yelled back.

I tried shoving the door with my right arm and shoulder before reaching the lagoon. It opened enough for a balloon.

"Hey!" Dave yelled.

I looked up and saw that the opening door had caused the airplane to wallow to the right. Dave corrected. I closed the door. The airplane veered left. The lagoon disappeared under the nose.

"Now! I think," Dave bellowed.

230

I shoved the door out and up and dumped the balloon over the sill. Whiskey tried to stick his head in the breeze. Slobber streamed back from his jowls. The "bomb" smashed against the leading edge of the wing behind my shoulder. The door slammed shut in the dog's face. The airplane slewed through the sky as Dave tried to keep up to the gyrations caused by the door. He banked left to watch the bomb drop.

"Never mind," I yelled.

He turned and looked at me. I pointed at the water spreading over the wing. "Oh no, we've been hit!" he roared. "You bombed our plane!"

I picked up the remaining balloon. "One more chance," I said.

We flew another circuit. This time Dave kept the Lake lined up. I didn't open the door until drop time.

"Now!" he yelled.

"How many points for the truck?"

I shoved the door and threw the balloon down and forward. It worked. I could see the red blob drop clear of the wing. "Bombs away!" I declared.

Dave turned left. I lost sight of the balloon below and behind us.

"I can see it!" Dave yelled excitedly.

I turned around and looked through the left rear window. I caught sight of the red dot descending earthward. Charlie's truck came into view. Charlie was beside it. He was struggling to open the driver's door. He succeeded and dove into the front seat just before the two-pound balloon smashed into the bed of the pick-up.

"Direct hit!" Dave whooped. "How many points for the truck?"

"I don't know. Maybe you'd like to ask Charlie."

"No thanks."

We circled and landed. When we taxied to The Flying Circus ramp, it was busy with the first wave of rental pilots getting ready to enter the contest. I was scheduled to fly with a student in one of our Cherokee 140s for a bombing run. I rode the right seat cradling our bomb load in my lap while the student flew. This time I only broke one bomb. I thought I could roll it off the wing but it broke on the step. Tossing the balloon behind the wing clear of the step worked but it didn't land anywhere near the lagoon.

After a few of these runs, I realized that hitting the lagoon with a balloon from a low-wing airplane at 500 feet was about as easy as throwing a gumdrop from a speeding car into a toilet bowl blind-folded. I thought the teams flying the high-wing aircraft might do better.

I took a couple of steaks-on-a-bun to Charlie in the infield during a lunch break. When I asked him the score, he showed me a blank clipboard. "The truck has been hit three times," he said. "I thought they were doing it for a joke at first, eh, but no one has come near the lagoon. I was thinking it would be safer to park next to the lagoon but it stinks too much."

I watched a couple of drops from the truck. They were all short of the mark. When I flew bombing runs that afternoon, I delayed the release. We got closer to the lagoon but it was obvious that this was not an exact science.

We had scheduled the contest until four o'clock. By three, there were still no lagoon hits. It wasn't from lack of trying. There had been a steady stream of aircraft in the bombing circuit all day. Between the two flying schools, Summer had collected two hun-

232

dred dollars for charity. Al Milton had done a brisk business with the barbecue and Dave Michelin had run out of donuts.

At three-thirty, Barney Swallow walked into The Flying Circus office carrying a metal bomb that looked real. It was mounted nose down on a block of wood. When he saw the surprised look on my face, he said, "It's a five-pound practice bomb from the British Commonwealth Air Training Plan. I've had it since World War II." His words whistled through his dentures. "The warhead contains paint," he explained, holding the bomb up by its fins and looking at it, "probably dried up by now. Anyway, I thought you should have a trophy for your contest so I had a little inscription made up and put on there."

He handed me the bomb. I read the metal tag pasted on the side: "Circus Water Bombing Contest - Best percentage Hits".

I wanted to ask the crusty old airport manager why he was at the airport on a day off but I caught myself in time. "That's very thoughtful of you, Barney. Thank you, but I have some bad news. There is half an hour to go in the contest and no one has hit the lagoon yet."

"Has nobody entered?"

"Plenty. More than 100 balloons have been dropped but no hits."

Barney looked around in disbelief. "Is the Cessna available?" he asked.

"Yes."

"You fly; I'll drop."

I knew that Barney had been a bomber pilot in the war. "The Cessna is not equipped with a Nordine Bomb Sight," I offered.

"And we're not bombing from 20,000 feet," he growled. He slowly extracted a wallet-on-a-chain from his back pocket, opened it and pulled out five dollars. He turned to Summer who was seated at the registration table and handed her the money. She gave him a plate of three water-filled balloons. "Are you bombing for the flying club or the Flying Circus?"

Barney handed one of the balloons back to her. He pointed at the remaining two on his plate. "Both," was all he said. Summer looked at me. I nodded to her that it was okay. Barney headed out the door. I scooped up the Cessna's logbook and keys, signed us out and rushed after him. Outside, Barney was hobbling like the old man he was toward the airplane. I caught up to him.

"What's the minimum speed on this crate, flaps down?" he asked.

233

"Sixty-five mph," I replied.

"On the bomb run to the lagoon, give me 70 mph and five hundred feet."

"Okay."

He stopped and turned to me. "Not okay. I want 70 mph and 500 feet exactly. No variations!" he barked.

"Yes, sir!" I replied.

"That's better. On the bomb run, use the rudder to change course on my command. When I say 'left', that's a one-degree turn; 'left, left' is two degrees. Got that?"

"Yes sir!"

"Let's go. The Huns are waiting."

Barney placed the balloons on the floor of the Cessna under the right front seat and hauled himself into the airplane. I checked the gas and oil, climbed in and fired it up. We took off from Runway 06. Barney stared at the target on his side of the airplane. I flew a left-hand circuit at 500 feet and lined up on the lagoon.

"Left, left, left!" Barney commanded as soon as I had established straight and level flight a mile back. I skidded the airplane left.

He said nothing until we were close to the target.

"Left, left!" he barked.

The way he had us headed, we were going to miss the lagoon well to the left. Then Barney unlatched his door and opened it against the slipstream with his left hand. The airplane reacted by turning right in a curving flight path to the lagoon. I didn't do anything to correct it.

My view of the target was disappearing under the nose when Barney picked up both of the balloons by their knots with his right hand. With his face pressed against the window, he held them over the opening at the bottom of the door. I could see that he was controlling our direction by varying the amount the door was open. We must have been right on top of the lagoon when he yelled, "Bombs away!" He slammed the door closed.

I banked right so he could watch the bombs out his side.

"Nice shot Ace," the controller in the tower said. "Do you want to continue in the right hand circuit for another run?"

"No, that's it," I replied. "We'll take a full stop. Was it a hit?"

"Double-barreled, dead centre!" the controller replied. "You're cleared to land."

234

"Bombs away!"

Chapter Thirty-seven

DOUBLE WHAMMY

On the Monday following the water bombing contest Henry and I were enjoying a coffee after opening the office. We were congratulating ourselves on the busy weekend. Leanne was opening the mail.

"I added up our revenue flying hours from the contest on Saturday," I said. "Fifteen point seven; that's pretty good for a bunch of short flights."

Henry nodded his head in agreement. "I know we'll get follow-on business from flying club pilots," he said. "I talked to them and they liked what they saw."

"They should. What other flying school offers donuts and jokes from a jolly dentist along with a water bombing contest?"

"I feel like business is really taking off."

Up to that point, Leanne hadn't said anything. "The extra flying from Saturday will just cover the increase on our loan payment," Leanne announced. She waved a bank notice.

"I thought we'd already covered it," I said.

"We had. This is another increase. The interest went up one per cent again. It's now thirteen and a half."

"Holy cow," I said, "we're working for the bank!"

"Bruce Stanwick's Archer will be ready soon," Henry offered. "Adding it to the line should increase our rental flying."

"We have to pay for the insurance on it first," Leanne reminded him.

We talked a little more about where the flying school was going. Despite the rising cost of our hangar loan, Henry and I were happy about the progress.

"At least we're still making the payments," Henry said. "When the loan is finished we'll laugh about battling this burp in the interest rates."

When we were done our coffees, Henry and I went outside to ready the airplanes for the day. We were pulling a Cherokee to the gas pump when our bank manager walked around the corner of the hangar.

"Hi, Horace," Henry said. "What brings you to The Flying Circus?"

Horace Green was a short, barrel-chested man. His shirt collar curled up in a vain attempt to find his neck. He was a nice guy but he talked through fat lips. He sounded as if his mouth was always full.

"Bad news," Horace said as he approached us. "My regional manager told me to reduce my high risk portfolio."

"What does that mean?" Henry asked.

"I'm calling your loan."

237

"I'm calling your loan." He chewed out the words quietly but clearly. He pulled out an envelope. "According to our agreement, you have 30 days to pay it off."

You could have knocked me over with a feather. I remembered Horace explaining the thirty-day recall clause when we had signed the loan application. Every bank included it in their lending but I had never heard of them using it.

"Did we miss a payment?" Henry asked.

"No, you've been good customers but I have to reduce my exposure by half a million." He handed the envelope to Henry.

"I don't understand," I blurted out. "If we're good customers, why dump us?"

"I don't have any choice," Horace said. He was clearly uncomfortable. Sweat was beading on his forehead despite a cool morning breeze. "The interest rates are making it harder for customers to pay so I have to cut the bank's risk."

As the reality of what he was saying sank in, I grew angry. "You raised the interest, Horace, and we pay it," I said sharply. "If that's a problem for you, then drop the damn rates."

Horace looked at Henry. "I need you to pay the loan off in 30 days or less," he said. He turned to leave.

"No chance of a reprieve?" Henry asked.

"No. I'm on my way to shut down a car dealer now. The interest rates will probably go up again. There'll be more loans called when they do." He turned and walked quickly toward the parking lot pausing only long enough to say, "Sorry guys."

We stood there stunned. "Wow, that's a kick in the head," Henry finally said. "I guess we have to go cap in hand to some other banks."

"It's a Catch 22," I replied. "We don't have time to go loan shopping and fly too. If we take the time, we'll lose business. Either way, the other banks are probably dumping loans. They sure won't want to pick up a client from a high risk list."

Henry kicked some gravel on the ramp. "I know what you're saying but I'm not going to let the bank shut us down without doing something," he said. "Let's talk to Leanne."

We walked into the office. "You two look like your dog ran away," she said with a smile.

Henry handed her the recall notice. "Bad news," he said. "Horace Green was just here."

238

She read the letter. "I guess he didn't want to take flying lessons," she said. The little joke helped ease some of the tension. "So now what?" she asked.

"We're fresh out of ideas," Henry said.

"I think it'd be a waste of time going to other banks," I said. "We don't know what to do."

"I do," she said, watching our reactions. We gave her blank stares. "We have a steady parade of successful people taking lessons and buying airplanes here. We treat them well and they go home happy. Looks like it's time to ask for a favor."

Henry looked at me and nodded his head in agreement. "It's a good suggestion," he said.

"I'd hate to do it but it might work," I replied.

"Good." Leanne stood up and checked the booking sheets. "We'll start with the Hathaways. I'll arrange for them to come early for their lesson tomorrow so you two can talk to them."

"I don't think we'll get anything," I said. "Retired couples are tight-fisted with money. They've already spent a lot with us for their new Archer only to have me wreck it. If they hear that we're on shaky financial ground, I'm afraid they'll take their business back to the flying club."

"I don't think they will," Henry said. "If they don't want to loan us the money, at least it'll be good practice to talk to them. Maybe they can offer some advice."

"They're retired hardware store owners, Henry. What can they tell us about running a flying school?"

"We won't know unless we ask," Leanne said.

I had to appreciate that they were determined to do something.

"Okay," I said. "Give them a call but I bet it doesn't get us anywhere."

Leanne spent the day drawing up an outline of our financial needs and projected income. Henry and I flew. It was hard to concentrate on the lessons while thinking about having our business pulled out from under us.

239

Chapter Thirty-eight

FREIGHT TRAIN

Susan should have been returning from an overnight trip to the far side of her territory when I headed home that night. I knew she'd be sympathetic and supportive about the bank problem. I pulled into the driveway. Lady was waiting in the spot where Susan usually parked her company car. The sun had set and the yard light had just clicked on. It was nearly nine o'clock. I guessed Susan's flight had been delayed.

I went into the barn full of hungry horses. I gave them all a pat, filled their water buckets and fed them some grain. I got grateful whinnies and nickers in return. Lady followed me into the house.

"You'd know what to do if the bank manager came here, wouldn't you girl?" The German Shepherd wagged her tail.

I turned on the lights and dug out the dog food. Lady wagged her tail some more. I fed her and then checked the fridge. My stomach was still churning from the events of the morning. I wasn't very hungry but I looked for something I could start in case Susan hadn't eaten. Eggs; they were quick. I found some bread and put it beside the toaster.

At ten o'clock, I turned on the news on the TV and sat down. The first story was about an airline crash in the far corner of the province. A file photo of the jet appeared on the screen behind the commentator. The airplane carried the markings of the airline Susan was using to fly home.

"Tragedy struck northwestern Ontario late this afternoon," the commentator said, "when an airliner crashed on takeoff in . . ." He named the town that Susan had been visiting. "Details are sketchy at this time but it is known that the airplane burst into flames on impact. There are no reports of survivors."

The blood drained from my head. I felt as if someone had hung me by my hands and cut off my feet. I was suddenly pale and dizzy but I got up and charged into the kitchen looking for the phonebook. I dialed the information number for the airline. It was busy. I

The first story was about an airline crash.

tried again and again. Then I tried the other numbers listed for the same airline. They were busy. Panic was growing inside me. There was no one to call in Susan's company. The headquarters and all the stores would be closed. Susan had all her contact numbers with her. Visions of the inside of that aircraft on impact flashed into my head.

I thought of calling the government Transport Department or the police or the airport at the crash scene. I desperately wanted to know that Susan was not on that airplane. I realized that if I could find those phone numbers, they would not tell me the passenger list. I looked outside. I wanted to see Susan walking up to the back door. It was dark. I couldn't think straight. I didn't know what to do. I called Henry. I tried to sound calm. It didn't work.

"There's been an airline crash," I blurted out.

"I know," he replied. "I saw the coverage on TV."

"Susan may have been on that airplane." My voice was cracking badly. "She should have been home by now . . . but she's not here . . . I tried calling the airline . . . but the lines are all busy . . . I don't know what to do." I was close to tears.

241

Henry's voice was calm. He spoke in measured tones. "I'm going to drive over to your place right now. If we don't find out anymore, we'll go to the International Airport. The airline will tell us what's happening. While you're waiting for me, keep trying the airline phone number and write a note for Susan in case she arrives when we're gone. You got all that?"

"Yes," I answered slowly.

"I'm leaving right away."

I tried the airline information number again and again. The line was constantly busy. Fearing the worst but not knowing was harder than I could ever have imagined. A tightness grew in my chest and a feeling of emptiness spread throughout my whole body.

Henry arrived 25 minutes after I had called him. It was a record time. I saw the headlights from his car flash across the barn when he swung into the driveway. I wanted it to be Susan's car.

I opened the outside door for him. "Find out anything?" he asked hopefully.

"Nothing. I keep getting a busy signal."

"Well, I can't think of anything better to do. Let's go to the International Airport. Did you leave a note?"

"Yes."

I turned to reach for my jacket. The telephone rang. It startled me so much I jumped. My heartbeat accelerated rapidly. It rang again.

"Do you want me to get it?" Henry asked. His voice pushed me into action.

"No," I said, slowly reaching for the receiver.

"Hel..lo?" I said. My voice cracked in the middle.

"Hi." It was Susan. Her voice sounded strained but it was definitely Susan. My whole body flooded with relief. I felt like someone had drenched me with a barrel of warm water. Initially, I couldn't speak. "Are you all right?" Susan asked quickly. "You sound strange. What's the matter?"

I didn't know whether to laugh, cry or scream. "W . . . where are y . . . you?" I sputtered.

"I wasn't going to say," she replied. "I have something important to tell you but maybe this isn't a good time."

In my relief, I tried to register what she was saying. Why wouldn't she want to tell me where she was? She wasn't making sense.

"I kn . . . know ab . . . bout the crash," I said. I struggled to regain control of my voice. "I thought you w . . . were dead. Did you miss

242

y . . . your flight?"

There was silence on the other end. I briefly thought someone who sounded like Susan was playing a cruel joke.

"That's what I wanted to tell you," she said slowly. The voice was soft but it definitely belonged to Susan. "I didn't take a flight."

"You don't know how relieved I am to hear your voice. We have to be the luckiest people on earth."

"I didn't fly out two days ago," she said.

Now I was really confused. She had called me the night before from the far side of her territory. It had been a normal conversation. She had said that she would see me tonight.

"Where are you, Susan?"

"I can't say but you should know I'm not coming home."

"You're not making sense," I said. "What's going on?"

She drew a deep breath and made her point. "I'm leaving you," she said. Her voice grew stronger as she spoke. "I cleared out all my stuff today except Cricket. I can't borrow a horse trailer until tomorrow. I'll take her then. I've arranged for the other horses to move up the road to the Schneiders so you don't have to worry about them." She was rhyming off an obviously rehearsed speech. "You may want to move Sunny there so he doesn't get lonely when you're working late. When I'm settled, we can talk about dividing up the rest of our property."

She paused for a breath.

At first, the realization of what she was saying didn't sink in. It was like dreaming about being run over by a freight train. Her brisk little speech was the train speeding in my direction. I was standing on the track but nothing was going to happen because it was a dream.

I didn't say anything.

"I'm sorry to tell you like this," Susan continued. "You sounded upset when I called but you had to find out somehow."

The train was closer. It was time to wake up to my normal life.

"Are you still there?" Susan asked.

"No, I'm not here," I said. "I'm somewhere else and I don't want to be there. There's a train coming and I want to get out of the way."

"You're talking nonsense," Susan said. "I don't like it when you're like this."

The vision of the train disappeared but the weight of it remained. I started to realize what was really happening. Susan was gone just as surely as if she had been on that flight.

243

It was like dreaming about being run over by a freight train.

"I've been thinking of this for a long time," she continued. "I don't want to continue living like two ships passing in the night. I'm sorry but I want to get on with my life."

As supervisor of a chain of ladies wear stores, Susan knew how to assess staff. She promoted the good ones and fired the ones who didn't measure up. Once she had made a decision, there was no turning back. I was being fired.

"You have your flying school and I have my career," she continued. "It's time to go our separate ways. I think it's best for both of us."

"Not taking that airline flight was the smartest thing you ever did," I said.

I looked at Henry. He was patiently standing by the back door with a puzzled look on his face.

"I'm glad you see it my way," Susan said.
"Sure. Thanks for calling."
"Are you going to be all right?"
"Yes," I lied.
"Okay, I'll call you when I'm settled."

Chapter Thirty-nine

BACK ON THE HORSE AGAIN

Henry and I were standing in The Flying Circus office the next day when the Hathaways pulled into our parking lot. Leanne was sitting at the flight desk opening the mail.

"That car has to be eight or ten years old," I said, "and their clothes look like they come from a bin at Good Will."

"They fooled us the first time we saw them," Henry replied.

"Yeah, who would have ever figured they'd buy an airplane?"

"Two airplanes," Henry corrected.

"Who's going to talk this time?" I asked.

"You're on the rebound; go for it."

Henry had stayed over with me the night before when I received the 'Goodbye' call from Susan. He had slept on the couch while I lay awake in bed with a rush of guilt running through my head. At first light I woke him up.

"Come one, let's go flying."

"What time is it?" he asked sleepily.

"Five o'clock. I want to go flying."

"What? The Hathaways aren't booked until ten."

"I know. We'll be back in time for them. Let's go. I'll buy you breakfast on the way. We'll take your car." I led him out to the Pinto. "I'll drive. You sleep."

"Are you sure you're okay?"

"I will be."

I drove him to an all-night diner and bought breakfast. "Early morning flying is like getting back on the horse after a fall," I explained. "A good friend of mine taught me that. You and I are going flying just for the fun of it."

He gave me a sleepy look over his coffee but didn't say anything.

We went to The Flying Circus, pulled out a Cherokee, gassed it up in the chilly morning air and took off into the sunrise.

"Now this is flying!" I declared with newfound enthusiasm. "This is why we started The Flying Circus."

246

Henry was waking up. He smiled. "You're right. We'll beat those bankers."

"You're damn right we will."

At ten o'clock, Glenn Hathaway held the office door open for his wife.

"Good morning," they said in unison.

"Good morning," Henry replied. "Thanks for coming."

"Hi, there," Leanne said.

"Good morning," I added from beside the coffee maker.

I poured coffee for everyone. The four of us sat at the ground school desks in the far corner of the office. I outlined what our bank manager had said.

Glenn and Margaret spoke at the same time.

"Let us cover the loan for you," Margaret offered.

"How much do you need?" Glenn asked. He pulled out his chequebook.

Henry and I looked at each other with our mouths open. We had rehearsed the pitch but not the response.

"The loan is $55,000," I blurted out. "Leanne wrote up a repayment plan for us based on projected business," I said holding out the loose leaf sheets.

Glenn ignored the offered plan and started writing a cheque.

"We can have a lawyer draft an agreement," Henry added quickly. "You could look at it and see what you think. We don't have to pay out the bank loan until the end of the month."

Glenn tore the cheque out of his book and handed it to me. "Pay the bloodsuckers off now," he said, "and don't bother with any thieving lawyers."

Margaret smiled and wrinkled her nose at the strong language. "Glenn can be so descriptive," she said. "He doesn't like bankers or lawyers."

"Consider our hangar rent as interest payments," Glenn continued, "and you can pay the principal by giving us instrument flying lessons and fuel."

I didn't reach for the cheque right away. "Your hangar rent is only $100 per month," I said. "That's only about two per cent a year. It's not enough."

"Consider our hangar rent as interest payments," Glenn said.

"It's two per cent at the beginning," Glenn said rising out of his chair, "but as the loan is paid down, the percentage goes up. It'll average out." He walked toward the flight desk with the cheque in one hand and his coffee cup in the other.

Margaret spoke. "If you think the interest payments are too low," she offered with a smile, "you could always raise the hangar rent."

Glenn handed the cheque to Leanne. "They're good instructors," he said to her, "but one of them needs to learn how to make better coffee."

Leanne accepted the cheque with a smile.

Margaret stood up. "I'm glad you let us help," she said. "Now I'm ready to go flying."

Henry and I were dumbfounded. We didn't know whether to laugh or give them a big hug. We didn't do either. The Flying Circus was back in business. We took them flying.